Footwear and footcare for adults

JANET HUGHES BA MCSP

Illustrations by Brenda Naylor

Funded by
'ACTION RESEARCH' — The National Fund for
Research into Crippling Diseases

DISABLED LIVING FOUNDATION, LONDON

First published 1983

© Disabled Living Foundation
  346 Kensington High Street
  London W14 8NS

ISBN 0-901908-43-6

British Library Cataloguing of Publication Data
Hughes, Janet
  Footwear and footcare for adults
  1. Feet — Care and hygiene
  I. Title
  617′.385   RD563

All information provided without legal responsibility

Produced by Time Graphics (Northampton) Limited, 20 Kingsley Park Terrace, Northampton, and printed by Stanley Hunt (Printers) Limited, Midland Road, Rushden, Northants.

CONTENTS

PREFACE

'When our feet hurt or are uncomfortable the whole body is affected'.
Agnes Cameron

Despite the fact that foot problems can have far reaching effects on posture, morale, and general well-being, footcare is often a neglected subject. An increasing proportion of the population are over the age of 65 – the age when disability and dependence are known to increase, and the inability to move about without pain combined with other problems – such as failing sight – can lead to isolation, confusion, dependence and depression. Some of the pain caused by movement can be relieved by proper footcare and footwear, but only in those who are lucky enough to receive the right treatment. In a survey of unreported illness carried out several years ago, almost half the people interviewed were suffering from some form of foot trouble and few of these people knew what to do about it. Since there are too few qualified chiropodists to undertake preventive care of the feet of elderly and disabled people, other health professionals need to be aware of the problems and their solutions. This book aims to provide the knowledge necessary to enable these professionals, many of whom visit patients in their homes, to give constructive advice on the subject of footcare and footwear. This is not a textbook for those already trained in the subject, but aims to broaden the education of others by explaining what treatments can help and how referrals are made.

Janet Hughes

ACKNOWLEDGEMENTS

As a physiotherapist – albeit with a special interest in feet – I have learnt an enormous amount during the preparation of this book, and would like to take this opportunity to thank all those experts who have helped by providing me with information and advice. It would not be possible to name them all, but one group to whom I must express my special thanks are members of the Society of Chiropody without whose help and support I could not have written the book. Their help is particularly appreciated in the chiropody and foot function chapters. Miss Mazie Collyer, Miss Judith Kemp and Mr Marcel Pooke – members of the Advisory Group – have been especially helpful.

I should also like to thank Professor J. C. Brocklehurst, Professor of Geriatric Medicine at the University Hospital of South Manchester, and Mr Leslie Klenerman, Consultant Orthopaedic Surgeon at Northwick Park Hospital, for their individual help with the medical and surgical chapters of the book. I am grateful to Miss Eirlys Rees, Chief Nursing Officer, British Red Cross Society, for her help in researching non-professional footcare.

The staff of the Disabled Living Foundation has again been very helpful and I am grateful to them all for their information and expertise. In particular I am indebted to Mrs Peggy Turnbull, the Clothing Adviser, for her help and guidance, and also to her team of voluntary workers, especially Miss Margaret Powell. Mrs Diana de Deney also deserves a special mention for editing the text and for coping with the task of keeping me to the printer's deadlines after I had started a busy, full-time job elsewhere.

I should like to thank all the members of the advisory group for their helpful support and advice throughout the project and for the time they gave up to read and comment on the many drafts involved. My special thanks go to Dr Bernard Lucas, Observer for Action Research, for his individual guidance.

I am again indebted to Mrs Brenda Naylor for taking 'time off' from her busy career to produce the illustrations which bring life to the text. I am very lucky to have had the continuing secretarial help of Mrs Penny Spencer and would like to thank her especially for her work.

Janet Hughes

MEMBERS OF THE ADVISORY GROUP

ADVISORY OBSERVER

Dr B Lucas
FFA RCS CIMechE

'ACTION RESEARCH' —
National Fund for Research into
Crippling Diseases

INTRODUCTION

Footwear and footcare for adults is the third publication about the feet and footwear to be issued by the Disabled Living Foundation (DLF). The first, *Footwear for problem feet* by M D England OBE FCLS, was written because the DLF's first survey, *Problems of clothing for the sick and disabled,* found that footwear caused more problems to the wearer than any other type of garment, and that families and professional staff agreed that this was so. *Footwear for problem feet* is therefore addressed to the wearers, who have difficulty in finding well fitting, comfortable shoes to suit their sore, tired and uncomfortable feet – not to those with acute problems of foot health requiring medical treatment. This book remains unique in its field.

DLF's second publication, *Footwear and footcare for disabled children* edited by Janet Hughes, was researched and compiled because the Advisory Panel to the DLF's clothing projects, including the Clothing Advisory Service, told the DLF that, in its opinion, insufficient work had been done on footwear in view of the extent of the problems footwear causes to disabled people of all ages, their families, and those who care for them professionally. In consequence, multi-disciplinary seminars were held, jointly with the Society of Chiropodists, on Footwear and Footcare for Disabled Children. These brought out the extent and severity of the problems, the frustration of the parents, and the unsolved question of how to get the information needed to parents and to others involved. *Footwear and footcare for disabled children* was therefore designed primarily for parents and non-medical staffs concerned, but also was aimed to increase the previously sparse information available to professionals and students in professions involved, but not specifically trained (as are chiropodists) in footcare and footwear advice. This book, too, is a first contribution in its field.

Footwear and footcare for adults, Mrs Hughes' companion study and DLF's third publication, again follows a series of multi-disciplinary seminars, this time held jointly with the Society of Chiropodists and the Department of Geriatric Medicine in the district where each seminar took place, on the similar problems experienced by adults. The contributions and discussion showed the substantial extent of foot problems among elderly people and its potentially disastrous consequences, not only to the individual, but to National Health Service and Social Services workloads and budgets. The problems affecting younger adult disabled people emerged also. Both sets of problems were shown to be aggravated by the shortage of professional chiropodists – the whole profession constituting only 25 per cent of the establishment required by the National Health Service alone. At the end of the seminars it was suggested that a book on this subject would be useful. The book would be intended primarily for the professions, other than chiropodists and doctors, caring for those with foot problems: that is, for nurses, therapists, residential and community social workers, care staffs, and supplies staffs. It was thought that these professionals, their students, voluntary bodies working in relevant fields and those who actually had the problems themselves would all find such a book useful.

The DLF therefore submitted an application to ACTION RESEARCH, the National Fund for Research into Crippling Diseases, which had already generously funded the research and writing of *Footwear and footcare for disabled children*. The Fund again agreed to give the grant required, and the DLF would like to acknowledge this gift with deep gratitude, which is equally felt by all concerned with DLF's clothing projects.

The DLF Trustees feel themselves very fortunate to have had the author, Mrs Janet Hughes BA MCSP, as project worker once more. The work needed turned out to be greater than originally estimated and Mrs Hughes' task much more difficult. In thanking her warmly they also thank the members of her advisory group (listed on page viii) who each commented in detail on successive drafts. The Trustees also much appreciate the important help given to Mrs Hughes by Professor Brocklehurst FRCP, Mr Leslie Klenerman FRCS, Miss Eirlys Rees CBE SRN, Chief Nursing Officer of the British Red Cross Society, and Dr Bernard Lucas, Special Adviser to the project appointed by the Fund. The Trustees also thank the illustrator of all the footwear books, Mrs Brenda Naylor, for her clear, explanatory line drawings.

Mrs Hughes, as she did before, has, as a part of her project work, assembled a travelling loan collection designed for professional training and information. This is available for hire from DLF and includes a range of footwear and hose for special needs, adaptations, aids, slides and lecture notes together with lists of manufacturers' names and useful addresses. Further particulars about this collection are available from the DLF's Clothing Adviser.

Footwear and footcare for adults is, like its predecessors, a pioneering book, first in its field. The Trustees hope it will be useful. They would again welcome and appreciate comments, suggestions and additional information which can be incorporated when the book is updated.

Feet still tend to be, relatively, an insufficiently considered part of the body, prone to mistreatment and to ill designed and damaging covering. The service and care they receive are still much in need of improvement. The DLF Trustees plan further publications, hoping to help with the problems.

W M Hamilton

1

The Foot

In the course of his evolution, man acquired the ability to walk upright on two feet and he has been doing so now for several million years (footprints of primitive man believed to be 3½ million years old have been found recently in larval cement in Tanzania). This transition from quadrupedal to bipedal locomotion has caused the foot to develop an arch – something unique in the animal kingdom. As a result, the foot is more advanced than the hand which has changed little since primates first began to climb trees. The foot, however, is not usually given as much consideration as the hand. Unless it is painful, a person is less aware of his foot, hidden as it often is inside a shoe. The area of the brain which controls the foot is much smaller than that which controls the hand. But the foot can still be used very skilfully as shown by the grace of a ballet dancer (see Fig. 1).

When someone is walking, the prime function of his lower limb is to support the trunk while he moves the other leg. When the walking surface is hard and flat – the pavement in a town, for example – this may seem a simple movement, but it is more complicated when the walking surface is uneven. In order to walk comfortably across rough surfaces, the foot must have two functions – first, it must be flexible so that it can accommodate uneven surfaces to give maximum support and balance; second, it must be capable of rigidity in order to transmit the thrust of the body to the ground in walking. The position and shape of the many joints of the foot enable it to perform these two opposite functions.

The many small joints concerned make the description of the anatomy of the foot complicated; it is also confusing, as different groups of professionals have different names for these joints (see

1

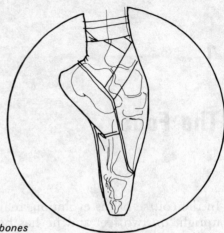

Fig. 1. Ballet dancer's foot bones

Fig. 2). For simplicity, only the main areas of movement and the functional part they play are described.

Movements in the foot and ankle

Before discussing the joints it is necessary to describe the various movements which the foot can make.

1. Dorsiflexion and plantarflexion

Dorsiflexion is the movement of the foot towards the front of the leg, plantarflexion (toe pointing) is the opposite (see Fig. 3).

2. Abduction and adduction

These are movements from side to side. In abduction, the front part of the foot moves away from the mid line of the body; adduction is the opposite, i.e. movement towards the other foot (see Fig. 4).

3. Inversion and eversion

These are turning movements. In inversion, the sole of the foot is turned inwards towards the mid line of the body; eversion is the opposite (see Fig. 5).

4. Pronation and supination

These are combinations of the above movements which occur when the foot is bearing weight. Pronation combines abduction, eversion and dorsiflexion; the inside edge of the big toe is turned in towards the ground. In supination, the foot adducts, inverts and slightly plantarflexes causing the inside edge of the foot to be lifted off the ground.

The muscles in the lower leg which act on the foot and ankle can be seen in Figure 6. The main muscle involved in each movement can be seen but there are many other small muscles which lie below those seen in the figure. A thick fibrous band *(extensor retinaculum)* passes over the top of the ankle and holds the tendons of the long muscles down to prevent them bowstringing as the muscle contracts.

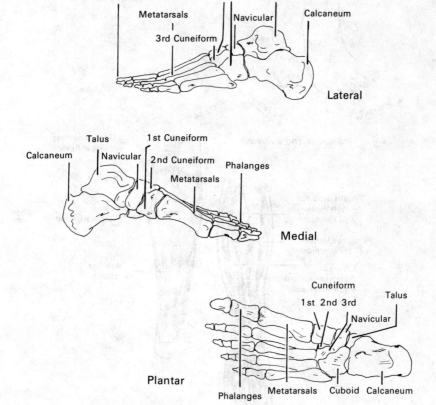

Fig. 2 Bones of the foot

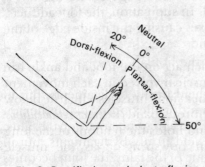

Fig. 3. Dorsiflexion and plantarflexion

Fig. 4. Abduction and adduction

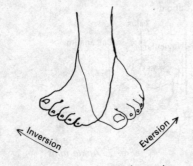

Fig. 5. Inversion and eversion

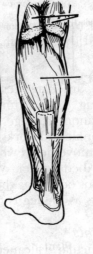
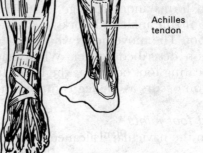

Fig. 6. Muscles acting on the foot

The joints

The ankle joint (see Fig. 7)
(between the talus, the tibia and the fibula)

The ankle is a very strong joint held firmly by ligaments, but in movement possible at this joint is dorsiflexion or plantarflexion and this movement occurs as the tibia and fibula rotate on the talus. The ankle is a very strong joint held firmly by ligaments, but in plantarflexion, due to the narrowing of the talus, the joint becomes less stable and most sprains occur in this position (see page 19).

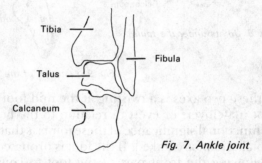

Fig. 7. Ankle joint

The joints under the talus
(sometimes called the subtalar joint – between the talus and the calcaneum)

There are three articular surfaces between the talus and the calcaneum (see Fig. 8). The function of these joints, if considered together, forms another hinge joint. This hinge is at an angle of about 45° to the ankle and works by transmitting rotations in the leg to the foot. The movements which occur here are pronation and supination described earlier. When standing, pronation of the weightbearing foot occurs as the lower leg is turned inwards and supination occurs as the leg is turned outwards (see Fig. 9).

The mid foot joints
(between the navicular, calcaneum cuboid and cuneiforms)

The articulations of these joints considered together form yet another hinge joint but with two axes. The combined movement

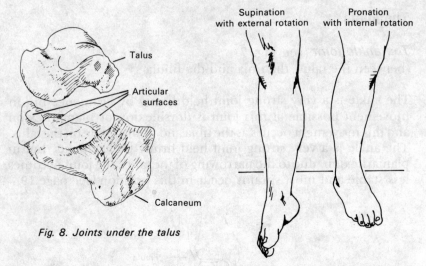

Fig. 8. Joints under the talus

Fig. 9. Function of the joints under the talus

about these two axes is a twisting at the mid foot level, so that the forefoot may invert or evert in relation to the heel and *vice versa*.

The functional significance of these joints is that the mid foot and the subtalar joint are linked. If the foot is pronated, these joints are loose allowing the front part of the foot to conform on uneven surfaces after the heel first touches the ground. If the foot is supinated, these joints are locked together firmly. The foot is thus made stable as full weight is transferred to it providing a rigid platform for the transmission of thrust to the ground.

The forefoot joints
(between the metatarsal bones and the toes (phalanges))

These articulations can also be described as hinge joints (see Fig. 10). Bending occurs at these joints as the heel leaves the ground during walking. At the push-off phase of walking, about half the body's weight may be placed on this forefoot area in contact with the ground.

Special features

The tightly packed fat in the heel and the fat pad beneath the matatarsal heads enable the foot to act as a shock-absorber so that

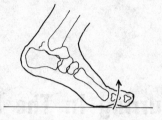

Fig. 10. Hinge action of the forefoot joints

the body is not jarred at every step. The pad under the metatarsal heads is held very firmly in place; it is attached both to the fibrous tissue which joins structures together under the foot (plantar aponeurosis) and the first joint in the toes. It is held taut when the toes are extended and thus takes all the weight during 'push-off' and reduces the effect of the shear forces on the plantar skin.

The plantar skin is the thickest in the body and, despite the ingenuity of the plastic surgeon, no flaps or grafts capable of withstanding the pressures exerted on the sole of the foot have so far been discovered. It also contains proportionately more sweat glands than any other part of the body.

This brief account of the way in which the foot functions shows its complicated structure. An abnormality in any of its parts, or any linked part in the entire body, can alter the way in which it is able to function.

2

Conditions Occurring In The Normal Foot

Pain in the foot can be disabling. The causes may be:

1. biomechanical (poor foot function due to impaired joint mechanics from degenerative changes, congenital deformity, paralysed muscles, hypermobile ligaments);
2. generalised diseases which affect joints in the fore- or hind foot such as rheumatoid arthritis or the neuropathy resulting from diabetes (see Chapter 4);
3. inadequate footwear;
4. local pathology in the foot.

Most conditions causing pain in the foot are simple and can be cured by relatively simple treatments. Sometimes the discomfort cannot be relieved by conservative means and surgery may be a solution. Surgery is indicated only occasionally for cosmetic or prophylactic reasons.

Conditions causing pain in the heel

Peritendinitis

This is a thickening or inflammation which can occur in the connective tissue surrounding the heel cord (achilles tendon). The area around the tendon becomes swollen and any movement which stretches the achilles tendon causes pain, for example, running and jumping. This condition – common in 'joggers', particularly those new to the sport, and in middle aged people playing games such as squash – may come on suddenly with an acute pain just above the heel.

Treatment   In the acute stage, ice will help to relieve the pain. Walking will be less painful if the achilles tendon is kept shortened by placing a wedge under the heel (see Fig. 11). This can be made temporarily out of newspaper but a foam material like plastazote or orthopaedic felt would be more comfortable. Wearing a sorbothane insole or heel pad (page 128) has a similar effect with the added advantage that it provides some shock absorption. The acute stage can also be made more comfortable by sticking pads of adhesive tape down each side of the tendon. Physiotherapy in the form of ultrasound may also help. Occasionally, the problem will need surgery to remove the thickened covering tissues surrounding the achilles tendon.

Recurrence can be prevented by advice on footwear and training, for example, runners should use thick-soled good quality running shoes and avoid training on roads – the yielding surface of a football pitch or woodland track is better.

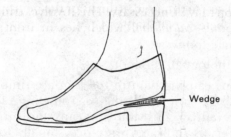

Wedge

Fig. 11. Wedge under heel for peritendonitis

Painful heel syndrome

Painful heel syndrome is analogous to 'tennis elbow syndrome' in its frequency and rather obscure pathological basis. Although a plantar spur may be present on X-ray, this can be an incidental finding and is not generally considered to be a cause of symptoms. The pain is usually on the inner side of the sole (plantar aspect) of the heel and is worse when someone with the pain first stands up after lying down or after long periods spent sitting. This condition can occur at any stage but it becomes more common after the age of 40.

Treatment One of the most common methods is the injection of hydrocortisone into the tender spot. Physiotherapy may be recommended, particularly ultrasound or short-wave diathermy, and chiropody can provide special insoles. The ready-made insole Rose Taylor (convex wedge insole, see page 127) which extends from beneath the long arch to the heel, is often helpful.

Heel bumps (winter heel)

This painful bump develops on the outer side of the heel next to the insertion of the heel chord (achilles tendon) (see Fig. 12). Teenage girls often notice this bump, caused by friction, when they start to wear high heels.

Treatment The symptoms may be improved by removing the heel stiffener from the shoe and placing a small wedge under the heel to raise the heel slightly as in peritendonitis (see Fig. 11). If the symptoms persist despite this and careful choice of footwear, a small operation may be necessary. This involves trimming the angle of the heel bone *(calcaneum)* which lies in front of the achilles tendon.

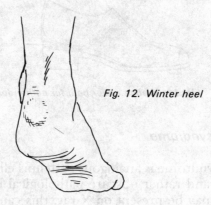

Fig. 12. Winter heel

Pain in the mid foot

Some people complain of a bony lump on the instep in line with the big toe. Slight prominence of a joint in the mid foot (that between the medial cuneiform and the metatarsals), is an individual variation which can cause pain if a shoe presses on it. The area becomes swollen and often a bursa forms to try to protect the bones from the pressure of the shoe.

Treatment Choice of footwear to avoid the area, e.g. a shoe fastened with a bar which comes above the problem area, can diminish the symptoms. An operation to remove the prominence is another solution.

Morton's metatarsalgia

This is a common cause of servere pain in the foot. The pain – a burning sensation which shoots to the tip of either the middle or the fourth toe – may start during walking. Rest can relieve the pain but the shoe may have to be removed before the pain disappears completely. Alternatively, the pain may be constant and, if particularly troublesome at night, may be relieved only if the weight of the bedclothes is removed or by letting the foot hang out of bed. It is caused by swelling of a nerve in the foot in the interspace between the third and fourth or second and third metatarsal bones. Sometimes a jerk can be felt as the forefoot is manually compressed; this is the swollen nerve popping in and out of the space between the heads of the metatarsals.

Treatment Chiropody treatment in the form of a toe prop (pad to spread the toes out) can relieve the pain. Careful choice of footwear and hosiery can also help. Shoes must be wide and hold the foot back in the shoe with laces or a bar so that the toes are not squashed together. If none of these remedies help, the only effective treatment is the surgical removal of the affected nerve; this is usually achieved through an incision in the sole of the foot as this skin heals more quickly than that on the top *(dorsum)*. Recovery after the operation is usually quite rapid.

Pain in the forefoot and toes

Hallux valgus

This is a sideways deviation of the big toe towards the other toes (see Fig. 13). It is associated with the development of a prominence on the inner side of the joint *(exostosis)* which then becomes protected

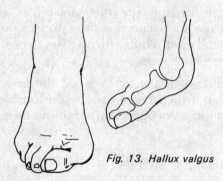

Fig. 13. Hallux valgus

by a bursa forming a bunion. Once the big toe has begun to deviate the process gradually worsens and the second toe is slowly forced to buckle into a hammer toe deformity (see Fig. 14). The cause of *hallux valgus* is not clear although hereditary factors may play a part. It is often found in a foot with a slightly shortened first metatarsal bone giving the first toe a structural weakness from the start and in those people who have a larger than average angle between the first and second metatarsal shafts. It is more common in women than men; this may be due to their different bone structure (wider hips applying a lateral force to knees and feet) or, which is more likely, it may be related to fashion footwear. Footwear is a major factor in the exacerbation of *hallux valgus,* and though probably only in those people with a susceptible foot shape (page 97).

Fig. 14. Hammer toe associated with hallux valgus

Treatment Correct choice of footwear is the first step in the treatment of *hallux valgus*. Although correct footwear cannot cure the problem, it might slow down its progression. The shoe must have a straight inside edge (see Fig. 15) and be fixed with a lace or bar so that the heel is held back in the shoe and cannot slip forward so that the toes are pressed into the shaped toe box.

Chiropody can help to relieve the symptoms by treating the soft tissue lesions (e.g. callosities) which are secondary, by making pads and shields (see page 68), and by inserting a balloon patch (see page 136). If the symptoms are severe, surgery may be recommended. Three main types of operations for this deformity are described briefly below, although each surgeon will use his own particular method.

The first operation, which realigns the big toe *(osteotomy)*, is the one which best preserves and maintains the use of the big toe. A cut is made in the far end of the first metatarsal bone and the head of the bone is slid sideways (see Fig. 16). This reduces the prominence on the inside edge and, at the same time, narrows the foot.

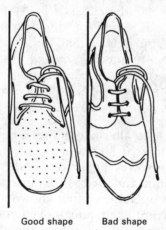

Good shape   Bad shape

Fig. 15. Shoe with straight inside edge

The second type of operation involves fixing the big toe joint in the correct position *(arthrodesis)* (see Fig. 17). This operation, usually carried out on the more grossly deviated big toes, allows the big toe to be completely realigned. The disadvantage of this operation is that the position in which the toe is fixed limits the possible variation in heel height. After an operation of this kind, it

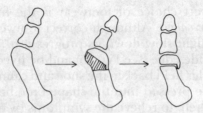

Fig. 16. Osteotomy for hallux valgus

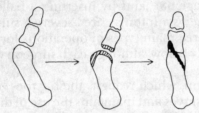

Fig. 17. Arthrodesis for hallux valgus

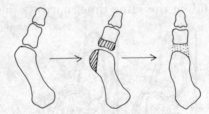

Fig. 18. Arthroplasty for hallux valgus

would not be possible to alternate between flat and high heels.

The third operation, which creates a new joint at the site of the painful big toe joint, involves the removal of the prominence on the inside of the big toe joint and the base of the first toe bone *(proximal phalanx)*. During this operation, often known as 'Keller's', the big toe is straightened completely and movement is maintained by bending the fibrous tissue which fills in the gap as healing takes place (see Fig. 18). Since the operation results in diminished stability and the big toe is left floppy and weakened, it is only performed on people who are not very active, for example, elderly people. The insertion of a silastic spacer, which fits into the base of the *proximal phalanx* and passes down the shaft of the first metatarsal, is a recent modification of Keller's operation. This preserves both the strength and the length of the big toe but carries a slight risk of infection.

Hallux rigidus

Hallux rigidus, as the name implies, is a condition in which the big toe becomes stiff at the metatarso-phalangeal joint. The upward movement of the big toe (dorsiflexion) is restricted making 'push-off' in walking difficult and painful. When the toe lacks this upward movement normal walking is impossible. Some people adapt their walking to roll their foot laterally away from the big toe as weight transference occurs, producing a characteristic lengthways crease in the shoe. Other people put extra strain on the end toe joint (the interphalangeal joint) causing the capsule to stretch and the tip of the toe to lift. The movement is limited by the development of a bony outgrowth *(exostosis)* on the top of the joint and bunion forms over this as it is rubbed by the shoe (see Fig. 19). This is due to degenerative changes *(osteoarthrosis)* but the reason for these changes is not always clear. It may follow a disorder of cartilage during growth or be caused by trauma. It could be caused, for example, by severe stubbing of the toe in youth or by repeated banging of the big toe on the inside of a pair of shoes which are too short (e.g. court shoes) (see page 99).

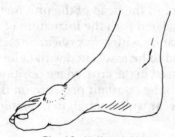

Fig. 19. Hallux rigidus

Treatment Chiropody appliances and footwear adjustments to modify the way in which weight is taken can help to relieve the pain. In the acute stage, physiotherapy in the form of ultrasound and manipulation is helpful. When the condition is chronic, the slight, remaining movement may cause pain (see Fig. 20). A rigid insole or rocker sole, which splints the toe straight and decreases the need to push-off, may help. However, these can be a hindrance to people in certain occupations, for example, those which involve much stair or ladder climbing, such as window cleaning. Similar operations to those carried out for *hallux valgus* may be suggested, either the

Keller's operation with or without the silastic implant or the stiffening operation *(arthrodesis)*.

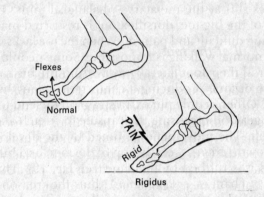

Fig. 20. Cause of pain in hallux rigidus

Bunionette (tailor's bunion)

This is a prominence of the head of the fifth metatarsal which, like *hallux valgus,* is associated with the formation of a small bunion. It may occur in association with *hallux valgus* or on its own. The cause is not known (it used to be associated with tailors in the days when this trade was practised in the crossed leg position (see Fig. 21)) and was probably due to the constant pressure on this bone. It can be difficult to get footwear wide enough to fit painlessly over a tailor's bunion.

Fig. 21. 'Bunionette'

Treatment Wide leather footwear stretched to fit over the bunion (see page ●) may be enough to relieve the condition. Surgery, involving cutting the fifth metatarsal bone at its neck and pushing this inwards to reduce the bump, may be recommended (osteotomy).

Pain in the ball of the foot

There are several causes of pain in the ball of the foot. It can be associated with toe weakness or deformity. For example, in diabetic neuropathy the toes do not work properly and their 'bent-up' position gives the under surface of the ball of the foot a convex contour putting extra strain in this area when weight is taken. The pain can also be due to degenerative changes or displacement of the fibro-fatty pad seen in rheumatoid arthritis (see page 38). Weight-bearing on the unprotected bone heads results in the formation of callosities which can cause pain and result in a feeling of walking on pebbles. Often this problem is due to a mixture of degenerative changes, poorly fitting footwear and, ultimately, weakness in the small muscles of the foot.

Treatment Chiropody to remove the callosities and provide insoles will help to relieve the pain. Many different types of insole or orthotic device (see page 69) can be made for this condition. They all work on the principle of allowing the unprotected heads to sink into a soft area incorporated into the device and redistribute the weight. Surgery, which may be suggested if the symptoms are severe, involves a diagonal cut in the ends of the metatarsal bones. This allows the head to be displaced upwards which can relieve the symptoms. If the condition is caused by rheumatoid arthritis all five toes may be involved and some form of forefoot reconstruction may be indicated. An operation of this type *(arthroplasty)* would

Fig. 22. Forefoot reconstruction for pain in the ball of the foot in rheumatoid arthritis

involve trimming the heads of all the metatarsals and stiffening of
the big toe to maintain stability (see Fig. 22).

Hammer toes

A hammer toe is one which has become fixed, bent at the joint
nearest to the foot and straight at the joint at the end of the toe (see
Fig. 23). It is often seen in the second toe associated with *hallux
valgus* (see page 12) as the pressure from a short shoe can cause both
these deformities. Too tight footwear can have a similar effect,
usually on the fourth toe, but all toes may be affected. Painful corns
develop on the fixed joints and sometimes a bursa forms on the top
as a result of pressure from footwear. Buying shoes becomes
difficult as extra depth is required to accommodate the bent toes.

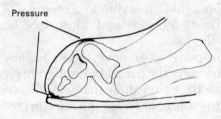

Pressure

Fig. 23. Hammer toe

Treatment Chiropody appliances can be made to hold the toe in a
good position while it is still flexible and chiropody treatment can
help to control the resulting corns and callosities. If the only
problem is the toe rubbing on footwear, the shoes can be made
comfortable by inserting a balloon patch (see page 136).

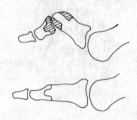

Fig. 24. Arthrodesis for hammer toe

Once the deformity is fixed, the only method of correcting it is by surgery. An operation can be performed to fix (arthrodese) the affected joint in the corrected position (see Fig. 24). It may be necessary to release the end joint also to stop it from sticking up once the other joint is straightened. Another operation involves shortening the toe to release the tension in the tendons acting on the toe and allowing it to fall into place without a lump.

Injuries

Sprained ankle

This injury to the lateral ligament of the ankle is caused by taking weight on the fully turned in foot (inverted). Usually the injury only causes a slight stretching of the anterior band of the ligament but even a slight strain may cause pain and swelling.

Treatment Ice packs, which will help to relieve the swelling, should be applied immediately after the injury. Mild sprains should be strapped and walking started as soon as possible. The strapping will be more comfortable if a pad of orthopaedic felt is cut to fit under the outside ankle bone (lateral *maleolus*). The bandage should extend from the base of the toes to just below the knee and should be applied with the ankle position at a right-angle to the leg and the foot slightly turned out (everted). To diminish the swelling, the foot should be elevated by placing it on a foot rest (see page 76) or, at night, by raising the end of the bed.

In the acute stage, physiotherapy may help to relieve the swelling, and ultrasound may be recommended. Later, exercises will help to strengthen the muscles around the ankle and prevent a re-occurrence; balance boards are particularly useful (see page 79).

More severely sprained ankles may need to be put into plaster for a short period followed by intensive rehabilitation.

Severe injuries and broken bones

Treatment of the more severe foot injuries will depend on which structures have been damaged. Not all broken bones will need to be treated in a plaster cast. The best treatment for a broken toe, for instance, is probably a comfortable shoe and a continuation of normal activity. If the injury is more severe, an operation to reposition the bones accurately (reduction) may be performed instead of immobilising the leg in a plaster cast since it is important to mobilise the foot as early as possible while healing takes place. One of the most important factors in all foot injuries is the prevention of swelling or its reduction once formed. Swelling will increase if the foot is allowed to hang down and adequate elevation when resting is important (see page 51). In hospital, the foot may be suspended in a tubular bandage (see Fig. 25) which both reduces swelling and keeps the foot in a good position.

Physiotherapy can help, first by reducing the swelling (see page 74) and secondly, by re-education in walking. Teaching the injured person correct movements of the foot even when walking with crutches will help to retain natural movements during recovery. The first step should always be taken with the uninjured foot to set the pace for the injured one. It is also better to walk with sticks than to walk with a limp without them, as limping may strain other joints and become an ungainly habit.

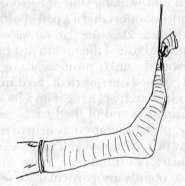

Fig. 25. Suspension of foot in tubular bandage following injury

Nail problems

Involution of nails

An involuted nail is one whose edge curves in towards the nail bed on one or both sides (see Fig. 26). This condition usually affects the big toe nail. One of the causes of this painful problem is tight footwear or hose which, by putting pressure on the nail plate, induces malformed growth.

Treatment   Mildly involuted nails may be difficult to cut, particularly at the edges which may be thickened. Chiropody treatment can help to thin the edges. Steel nail braces can be made for more severely affected nails.

Fig. 26. Involution of nails

Ingrown toenail (onychocryptosis)

An ingrown toenail, another cause of pain in the big toenail, is caused by rough edges of nail becoming embedded in the skin as the nail grows. The irritation this causes results in inflammation, pain and swelling; in addition, the inflamed area usually becomes infected. The main causes are faulty nail cutting, narrow footwear and excess sweating (page 28). Two methods of nail cutting are at fault (see Fig. 27). First, if the nail is cut too short the tissue below is allowed to bulge and, as the nail grows, it digs into the bulge, Secondly, if the nail is cut down at the sides, it becomes deeply embedded in the skin making further cutting more difficult and increasing the risk of leaving a rough splinter behind.

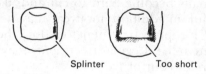

Splinter   Too short

Fig. 27. Faults in nail cutting which can lead to an ingrowing toenail

Treatment   Simple chiropody techniques may be able to isolate and remove the rough portion of nail. If the inflammation is acute, minor surgery may be necessary to cut out a small wedge of nail and nailbed. Proper drainage of the nailbed can be achieved in this way, so that the inflammation subsides and the nail cannot regrow to its original width. In severe cases of infection, the whole nail and nail bed may need to be removed. Advice on correct nail cutting and footwear can prevent recurrence.

Extra thickening of the nail (hypertrophied nail) – onychauxis

Sometimes toenails, often only the big toe, grow very thick and become difficult to cut. Brownish staining of the base of the thick nail (nail plate) is often evident. Extra thickening is caused by damage to the growing part of the nail. Several factors may cause this – for example, injury, footwear pressing on uncut nails or some infection. If left uncut, these nails can become very painful.

Treatment In mild cases, cutting can be made easier if the foot is washed first so that the nail is softened slightly, or if the top surface of the nail is filed with an emery board or nail file to reduce the thickness before cutting.

To ensure that the nail is not compressed, there must be enough room inside the toe box of the shoe to allow the toes to move freely.

Severe cases will need regular chiropody treatment to keep the excessive thickening under control. Sometimes the nail may be removed (avulsed).

Ram's horn nail (onychogryphosis)

In this condition the nail becomes thickened and deformed, and looks rather like a ram's horn (see Fig. 28). This is caused by the nail growing faster on one side than the other. The condition is usually caused by severe injury, for example, a bad stubbing of the nail, or it may be due to infrequent nail cutting. Once the condition is present, the nails become hard to cut and, if left untreated, will become painful; in addition, footwear may no longer fit.

Treatment Chiropody treatment to reduce the size of the nail will give immediate relief. Regular treatments may be needed to keep the growth under control.

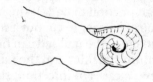

Fig. 28. Ram's horn nail

Skin conditions

Rashes

Rashes affecting the feet can produce intense irritation and itching. These rashes may be caused by local irritation, e. g. allergy to rubber soles or shoe uppers, a fungus infection or they can be part of a more widespread condition like eczema (page 25).

Rashes on the feet are fairly easily distinguished by their distribution (see Fig. 29).

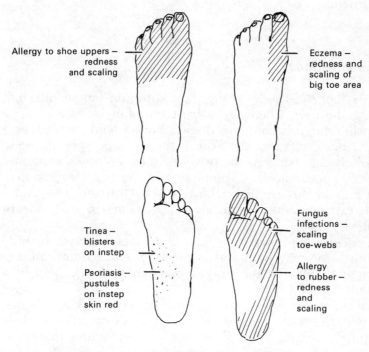

Fig. 29. Rashes on the feet

Allergy

Allergic contact dermatitis presents a symmetrical picture and appears over the area of contact, so that red, itchy soles with a relatively untroubled instep may indicate a reaction against rubber soles (e.g. in slippers). Similar symptoms on the top of the foot avoiding the toe webbs might mean allergy to the chromate used in the tanning of shoe uppers or to shoe dye.

Buying shoes of different material will usually solve these problems although, occasionally, shoes free of the particular allergen will have to be made specially.

Another fairly common allergy is one to washing powder. Though this affects most clothing, it tends to appear on the feet as the sock is pressed firmly into the skin by the shoe. If this is the case, areas touched by the top of socks or other elasticated garments in contact with the skin will also be affected. This problem can usually be solved by changing the washing powder and careful rinsing of the garment.

Fungus infections

Athlete's foot *(tinea pedis)* is the most common fungus infection affecting the foot. There are a variety of fungi which may be responsible for this common disease but all tend to produce a similar clinical picture. The skin in the webs between the toes, particularly that between the two little toes, becomes white and sodden in appearance and scaling occurs; the skin may also itch. Sometimes in this condition blisters occur on the instep, and another variety produces a chronic scaling of the skin and creases of the soles.

Soft corns due to macerated skin in the cleft between the little and fourth toe may be mistaken for fungus infections and it is important to identify the fungus precisely with the help of a bacteriologist.

Since athlete's foot is spread by touching infected skin on floors, bath mats, towels, socks or shoes, it is often contracted in communal changing areas, for example, in swimming pools.

Antifungal ointment will be prescribed but prevention of the spread of the infection is important. In communal areas, regular cleaning and foot baths will help and, at home, walking barefoot and sharing towels or shoes and socks should be avoided. Towels and socks should be washed separately and treated with a sterilising agent. Wearing socks in bed will prevent the infection spreading to the feet of one's partner.

Eczema

Eczema can occur in the foot and produces an itchy, vesicular rash. On the sole, it produces a lumpy appearance because the vesicles are under the thick skin on the sole.

Any skin condition affecting the foot will be aggravated by poor foot hygiene and great care must be taken when washing and rinsing hose as soap particles left in stockings and socks can irritate. Where rashes cause irritation, footwear must be chosen with great care to try to avoid sensitive areas. Sometimes, soft leather uppers may help. Socks of different material, for example, cotton rather than synthetic, can be more comfortable (see Appendix II), as people with eczema may also have an allergy to synthetic fibres.

Callosities and corns

Callosities, simply excess thickening of the skin, are the body's reaction to mechanical pressure or friction. A corn is a cone of more dense callosity which usually forms over a bony prominence, for example a small joint in the toes. As people get older the skin tends to lose its elasticity and the fibro-fatty padding under the skin gets thinner. Thus activities or pressures which would cause no symptoms in young skin may cause painful problems in older people.

Pain-free callosities Pain-free callosities do not need any attention. Removal of these may actually make the situation worse as the body may react by producing even thicker callosities.

This type of thickened skin can be kept under control by regular, careful use of a pumice stone or chiropody sponge after bathing (stones and sponges should be kept clean and dry and be used only on healthy skin as they could harbour infection). The skin can also be rubbed gently with disposable emery boards and even fine household sandpaper when the foot is dry; rubbing with these presents less risk of infection than rubbing with sponges and stones. Rubbing an ordinary hand cream into the feet regularly will help to keep the skin soft and supple.

Painful callosity Pathological callosities can be extremely painful and give the sensation of walking on stones in the shoe. This type of thickened skin is a symptom of excess pressure and removal by the chiropodist will relieve the pain but will not solve the basic problem. Continuation of the pressure which resulted in the formation of the callosity will undoubtedly cause it to re-occur. Removing the excess pressure or friction will encourage the skin to return to its usual state and the thickened skin will be shed in the normal process of skin cell turn-over. The chiropodist will be able to advise on the cause of the callosity and the type of footwear which will, by relieving the pressure, cure the problem.

Home treatments Rubbing with a pumice stone or chiropody sponge (as described above) is recommended, but commercially available preparations designed to remove callosities should be used with extreme care. Some of these contain caustic substances which act on the callosity by virtually burning it off. If these preparations are allowed to come into contact with unthickened skin, they can cause quite severe burns which can become infected and take a long time to heal.

Soft corns These occur on moist skin so that the corn cannot harden; they can be extremely painful. Soft corns often appear between the fourth and fifth toes (see Fig. 30); they may be caused by a small bump on the tip of the toe bone (proximal phalanx). Treatment by a chiropodist and careful attention to the fit of shoes can be helpful, but sometimes the surgeon may have to remove the underlying bony prominence.

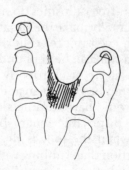

Fig. 30. Soft corn between fourth and fifth toes

Chilblains

Chilblains are red and swollen areas on the toes and heels or other extremities which can be very itchy. They occur in cold weather and are caused by an abnormal reaction of the blood vessels to changes in temperature.

Chilblains occur less frequently now that central heating is more widespread but can be an uncomfortable problem for some people. The best way to prevent chilblains is to keep the whole body warm. Warm footwear is essential (page 155) but, if the legs are cold, the heat will dissipate as the blood circulates. Warm hose (page 155) or trousers should therefore be worn but clothing must not be tight as this will constrict the circulation and increase the problem. If the feet get very cold, they should be warmed gradually to diminish the chance of chilblains occurring. The application of hot water bottles or other sources of direct heat should therefore be avoided; pre-warmed footwear and hose can warm the foot (see page 157).

Blisters

Blisters are a result of unusual friction on a softer area of skin, for example, a new pair of shoes rubbing the back of the heel. The body's reaction to this friction is to make a cushion of fluid between two layers of skin. Blisters can be very painful, but should not be burst as this will increase the risk of infection. However, it is safe to burst the blister with a sterile needle after 24 hours when new skin has formed underneath as long as the skin covering it is left. If the source of the friction is removed, the blister will usually heal very quickly.

New shoes that cause blisters can be made more comfortable if the area of the shoe which rubs is softened slightly by gentle hammering; also sandpapering the rough areas inside a shoe like a seam can take off the rough edge. If blisters occur as a result of unusual activity, such as a long walk or extra sporting activity, two thin pairs of socks (the outer one must be a size larger) instead of one thick one should be worn; this will help to cut down the friction as some of the friction force occurs between the two layers of socks. Training for such activities by starting gently and building up the activity gradually over several weeks is a more satisfactory way of avoiding these problems, although the skin over the affected area can be toughened in advance by daily applications of surgical spirit in the two or three days preceding the activity.

Excess sweating (hyperhydrosis)

The skin of the sole of the foot has a large number of sweat glands which normally produce up to half a pint of sweat a week. Sometimes these glands are overactive and excess sweating results. Skin kept moist by sweat provides an ideal environment for fungus and other infections. Scrupulous attention to foot hygiene, wearing clean socks and wearing sandals to allow ventilation, are the best ways to keep the feet dry and odour free. The material of which the footwear and hose is made is important. If both are made of non-porous synthetic materials the sweat will remain in contact with the skin. Shoes with leather uppers and socks which are made of a material which will help to transfer moisture away from the skin (wicking, see page 150) will be more comfortable. Commercially available anti-perspirant sprays and powders can also be helpful and chiropodists may be able to supply special insoles.

Cramp in the leg or foot

Cramps can be caused by excessive exercise, impaired circulation or a low calcium level in the blood. They are common in women in the later weeks of pregnancy and often occur in those who stand for long periods particularly in ill-fitting or high-heeled shoes. Elderly people with poor circulation may get cramp as well as those who smoke as tobacco causes spasms in the small arteries. Cramps are worse at night when the blood pressure and the pulse decline during rest and the circulation is slower.

Treatment The foot should be massaged until the cramped muscles relax. Sometimes standing up will bring quick relief. Warm baths and gentle exercise may also be helpful. Medical treatment includes calcium and Vitamin D or drugs which dilate the blood vessels.

3

The Abnormal Foot

Deformities in the foot can be present at birth (congenital) or occur as a result of childhood conditions, for example, arthritis (juvenile chronic arthritis), cerebral palsy, trauma or poorly fitting shoes worn while the foot is growing.

Some congenital deformities, which can be treated simply in early childhood, have little effect on adult life, for example *metatarsus varus* (when the forefoot curves inwards towards the other foot). Others will need surgery to correct the position of bones for normal growth. Further problems occur if full correction cannot be achieved early, as the bones will grow in the deformed position leading to abnormal function in adulthood.

Some deformities which result from childhood disease may be corrected by surgery to soft tissues during growth, for example flat foot caused by muscle imbalance in cerebral palsy. In other cases, operations to bones may be necessary which cannot be carried out during childhood because of possible damage to the growing points of bones *(epiphyses)*.

Treatments which are carried out to correct deformity in childhood are not described in detail (see Appendix IV for further reading on the subject) but are mentioned in relation to the subsequent problems which may occur in adulthood.

Common deformities have been given names which describe the resulting abnormal position of the foot position without lengthy description. Several of these are described below.

Varus and valgus (see Fig. 31)

These terms are used to describe deformities that occur in the body. *Varus* refers to deformity towards the mid line and *valgus* to

29

deformity away from the mid line; for example, *hallux valgus* when the big toe deviates away from the mid line. When considering the whole foot, the description is again complicated by the many joints involved. *Valgus* is now a pronation deformity (looking at the foot from behind, the heel is seen to point outwards (evert)). *Varus* is the opposite and is associated with a supination deformity.

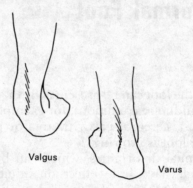

Fig. 31. Varus and valgus

Equinus and calcaneus

Equinus refers to a deformity in which the foot or part of it is fixed in plantar flexion so that the heel cannot be put down to the ground when standing (someone having this deformity appears to be walking permanently on tip toes) (see Fig. 32). In *calcaneus,* the foot or part of it is fixed in dorsiflexion so that the front part of the foot cannot be put down to the ground when standing (see Fig. 33).

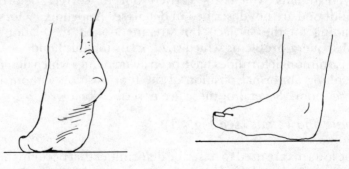

Fig. 32. Equinus   *Fig. 33. Calcaneus*

Flat foot *(pes planus)*

In this condition the medial long arch of the foot appears to be flatter than normal (see Fig. 34). It is very common, occurring naturally in some races but rarely needs treatment as the height of the arch has been shown to bear no relationship to the functional capacity of the foot as long as the foot is mobile.

All children appear to have flat feet when they start to walk; this is due, first, to the presence of a fatty pad which disappears as the child walks more frequently, and secondly, to the stance he or she adopts when walking in the early years (legs apart and turned out with feet rolled in). Even when walking is established, the foot may appear flat because of positions of the lower limb, such as knock-knees *(genu valgus),* which normally correct spontaneously with growth.

Flat foot in older children or adults is rarely due to a true flattening of the arch although this may occur in people who are loose-limbed (hypermobile) but to an inrolling or pronation of the foot *(valgus)* which may also give rise to a secondary *hallux valgus* (see page 11). The flat foot may also be caused by an underlying neurological disorder causing muscle imbalance, for example, cerebral palsy or multiple sclerosis.

Flat foot can be associated with pain and stiffness. Painful flat foot may be due to a bony abnormality, muscle strain, infection or arthritis (see page 39). Pain combined with stiffness may also be due to a bony abnormality, for example, peroneal spastic flat foot (see page 32). Stiffness alone may be the result of arthritis in childhood (juvenile chronic arthritis).

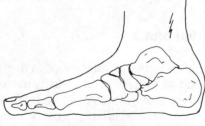

Fig. 34. Flat foot

Treatment If the flat foot is flexible (mobile) and pain-free, no treatment is necessary. The types of flat foot which may require treatment are those which are painful, stiff, excessively mobile or are caused by some neuro-muscular or skeletal abnormality.

Treatment will depend on the underlying cause of the deformity. Infection can be treated by drugs; bony abnormality either by immobilisation in a below knee walking plaster for a short period or surgical removal of the abnormality as in peroneal spastic flat foot (see below).

Where the flat foot is due to a general condition such as cerebral palsy, the cause itself cannot be influenced and the foot must be corrected by other means. A number of appliances and adaptations to footwear are prescribed to try to correct flat feet – Thomas heel, medial wedge, valgus insole, heel cup (Rose Schwartz, Helfet), T-strap and iron (for descriptions, see page 130). These adaptations and appliances can make the condition more comfortable or decrease shoe wear, but it is difficult to control this deformity with shoes or appliances as the position tends to re-occur inside them.

Physiotherapy may be advised to help to relieve the pain or to teach the person to walk in a different way. Although it has been proved that the small muscles of the foot have no effect on the arch of the foot, they can affect the way the weight is taken on the foot during walking. Faradic foot baths to retrain the use of these muscles can be very effective and relieve pain. Ultrasound may be used on local tender areas.

If the deformity is progressing either by increased pronation or the start of *hallux valgus,* surgery may be necessary. In children, operations to balance the muscles can be helpful. When pain and deformity are resistant to other measures, adults may need more extensive surgery to fix the bones in a good position; this operation, however, leaves the foot stiff which can also be a handicap.

Peroneal spastic flat foot

This condition, which occurs in adolescence, is due to a congenital abnormality in the tarsal bones and results from the failure of the individual tarsal bones to separate completely during embryonic development. The commonest variety is a bony bridge between the calcaneum and the navicular (see Fig. 35). The condition does not produce symptoms until adolescence because these bridges are cartilaginous at first. They gradually harden *(synostosis)* with growth, and the symptoms appear when extra activity – such as prolonged standing or marching – stresses the joints which are now rigid. The symptoms are pain in the heel and stiffness of the foot with a marked spasm in the muscles which turn the foot outwards (peroneal muscles) caused by the pain (reflex spasm). These symptoms could also be due to protective spasm caused by an inflammatory condition in the mid-tarsal or subtalar joint.

Treatment An insole may be used to support the arch and prevent stress to the joints or it may be necessary to have a six week period of immobilisation in a plaster cast to relieve the pain and relax the spasm followed by the protection of an inside iron and outside T-strap (see page 125). Surgery may be necessary. If the problem is discovered while the foot is still growing, it may be possible to cut out the bar. In the mature foot, an operation can be performed which changes the line of weight bearing (osteotomy). This is achieved by removing a wedge from the inside of the heel bone.

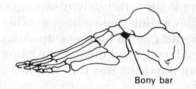

Bony bar

Fig. 35. Bony bridge between calcaneum and navicular

High arched foot *(pes cavus)* (see Fig. 36)

This deformity may be present at birth (congenital) or may be caused by neurological conditions. The inside arch, and in severe case, the outside arch too, are abnormally high and there may be associated deformities of the toes and heels. The toes tend to claw and the heel may tilt inwards *(varus)*.

The congenital form, often inherited, is rare compared with the same deformity due to other causes. Usually, both arches are high but there is no associated toe deformity.

High arched foot may not be noticed when the child is young because of the extra fat pad in babies' feet; it may not be diagnosed until the parents seek advice about how to combat excessive shoe wear (which can be the result of walking with this deformity), or about the type of shoe to fit over the deformity.

This deformity is often associated with neurological conditions, for example, peroneal muscular atrophy or spina bifida. Like the congenital form, excessive shoe wear may be the first sign that something is wrong or the child may fall repeatedly due to the underlying neurological condition.

Fig. 36. High arched foot

If *pes cavus* passes unnoticed during childhood, the extra weight involved as the child grows will increase the abnormal loading on the metatarsal heads leading to pain and the formation of callosities in adolescence (see page 25). The toe deformity may become fixed and rub on the upper of the shoe causing callosities in that area.

Treatment   In mild cases, the only treatment necessary will be advice on shoe fitting and ways of minimising shoe wear (see page 94). Shoes should open a long way down so that they can be easily adjusted over the high instep (see page 88). Extra depth in the toe box will prevent the deformed toes rubbing on the top of the shoe (see page 96).

A supportive insole with a pad behind the metatarsal heads may help by increasing the load-bearing area, thus spreading the load more evenly.

In some cases, an operation may be necessary. While the foot is still growing, operations on the ligaments and short muscles of the foot can help to correct the position. In addition, the tendons of the muscles which make the toes bend may be transferred to make them straighten the toes. If the heel bends inwards, an operation on the heel bone may be necessary to realign the heel.

When the bones have stopped growing, more extensive operations can be performed to correct the deformity. These may involve removing a wedge of bone from the apex of the arch (see Fig. 37) or, if the deformities are more complicated, some joints may be fixed in a good position.

Club foot *(talipes equinovarus)*

A club foot deformity is one in which the foot is fixed pointing downwards and inwards *(equinus and varus)* (see Fig. 38). The cause of the deformity is not known, but it can occur on its own or secondary to other handicapping conditions, for example, spina bifida.

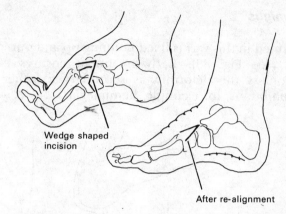

Fig. 37. Operation to remove a wedge of bone from the apex of the arch

When it is the primary condition, club foot can usually be corrected completely, although an operation may be necessary to achieve this. The feet and lower legs may remain rather small; this is most noticeable when the club foot has been one-sided. It is due to the fact that the deformity starts in the womb and the growth of the affected foot and calf muscle may never catch up with the unaffected leg. Odd-sized shoes may be recommended (see page 104).

The effect of treatment is less predictable when the club foot occurs secondary to other conditions. Surgery may be postponed to cut down the risk of recurrence and there is often some residual deformity. The achilles tendon may remain slightly tight so that it may be more comfortable to walk in shoes with a slight heel or special footwear may be needed.

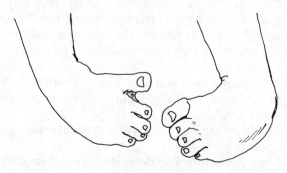

Fig. 38. Club foot

Calcaneo valgus

A foot deformed in this way is fixed pointing up and out *(calcaneus* and *valgus)* (see Fig. 39). Early treatment ensures complete correction unless the deformity is secondary to other neuro-muscular conditions, for example, hemiplegia.

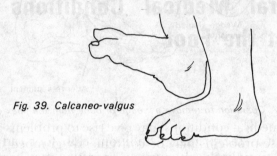

Fig. 39. Calcaneo-valgus

Rocker bottom foot (congenital vertical talus)

Rocker bottom foot is a very apt description of this deformity as the foot appears convex on the under surface (boat-shaped). The hind foot is fixed pointing downwards and the forefoot is caused to roll inwards. It is a rare deformity but always needs early surgical correction.

Toe deformities

Most toe deformities present at birth improve with time and need no treatment. Appliances made by chiropodists will help to keep deformities to a minimum while the foot is growing. If a curly toe needs to be straightened surgically, the operation will usually be put off until the bones have stopped growing to prevent damage to the growing ends.

If the little toe is deformed and over-rides the other toes, buying and wearing of shoes may be difficult and corrective surgery may be needed.

Sometimes the toes are webbed (syndactyly) and may need to be separated by plastic surgery.

Congenital toe deformities seldom lead to major problems in adult life.

4

General Medical Conditions which Affect the Foot

Certain medical conditions may give rise to problems affecting the feet. These problems may be conveniently grouped into:

1. deformities resulting either from diseases of the joints or of the central nervous system;
2. inadequate blood supply resulting from disease of the blood vessels of the feet or legs;
3. damage to the skin of the feet as a result of altered sensation due to peripheral nerve disease;
4. swelling due to abnormal fluid balance.

The problems posed by each of these main groups are different. Splinting and appropriate footwear are necessary to try to prevent, and to accommodate, deformities. Inadequate blood supply will increase the risk of pressure sores and also the risk of infection during surgical or chiropodial treatments. Feet with altered sensation need special care to protect them from inadvertant damage; swelling may necessitate special shoes.

Rheumatoid arthritis

Rheumatoid arthritis is a condition in which inflammation of the joints occurs as part of a widespread systemic process. It can occur at any age and after an acute onset follows an uneven pattern of remissions and flare-ups.

The cause is not known though it is probably associated with a disorder in the body's mechanism to resist disease. Specific treatment is not yet available but there are many non-specific treatments which may relieve the painful symptoms. Because the disease has remissions, many so called 'cures' are apparently successful for a while until the symptoms return.

The joint involvement in rheumatoid arthritis is usually symmetrical. The joint space becomes narrow, erosions occur in the ends of the bones and the tissues become thickened. Movement becomes stiff and painful, particularly after resting. In the foot, there are two common patterns of involvement.

Involvement of the forefoot

Disease in the joints of the forefoot results in a clawing deformity of the toes which may progress to partial dislocation (subluxation) (see Fig. 40). This is caused by a combination of the disease process in the toes and abnormal weight bearing. Forward migration of the fatty pad which usually forms a cushion under the heads of the metatarsals may accompany this deformity (see Fig. 41).

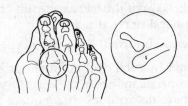

Fig. 40. Subluxation of second toe

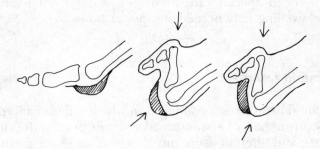

Fig. 41. Migration of fatty pad in rheumatoid arthritis

This deformity of the toes is often combined with *hallux valgus* (a sideways drifting of the big toe, see page 11) and bunions may form.

Toes deformed in these ways cannot bear any weight and the extra weight involved in standing or walking is taken on the metatarsal heads. Walking on the uncushioned bone ends gives a sensation of walking on marbles which can in turn lead to painful callosities (see page 25). Occasionally, poor skin condition leads to breakdown of these areas and ulcers develop.

Involvement of the back part of the foot (hindfoot)

When disease occurs in the joint beneath the talus (see page 5), the heel tends to twist outwards on the ankle causing the front part of the foot to roll inwards *(valgus)* (see Fig. 42). Once this deformity starts it is accentuated by the body weight bearing down on it. The effect of this is to flatten the inside arch and change the pattern of weight-bearing under the sole.

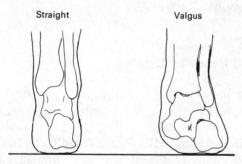

Fig. 42. Heel straight and in valgus when the back part of the foot is involved in rheumatoid arthritis

Other problems

Nodules underneath the heel or on the achilles tendon may present difficulties which will require special footwear incorporating soft insoles.

Apart from the deformities, inflammation may occur in the blood vessels *(vasculitis)* which may make the skin very fragile and liable to break down following fairly mild trauma. This increases the risk of infection.

Occasionally the nerves are affected; if they are, burning sensations and altered touch sensation may make any kind of footwear uncomfortable.

Treatment

If rheumatoid arthritis involves the foot, good foot management is important. People with rheumatoid arthritis will be under the care of medical practitioners who will control drug treatment and advise on surgery when necessary (see page 17). Physiotherapists will stress the importance of exercise and can offer pain-relieving faradic foot baths (see page 79). Chiropody can also be helpful by treating the callosities, corns and ulceration and by providing appliances to redistribute the pressure (see page 69).

Footwear must be lightweight and soft with extra depth to accommodate both deformity and padding. A number of ready-made shoes have been specially designed to fulfil these needs (see Chapter 8 section 1(i) page 107).

Psoriasis and Psoratic Arthritis

Psoriasis is a general skin condition which produces patches covered in silvery scales. Psoriatic arthritis is a type of arthritis which can occur in people who suffer from psoriasis. The joint involvement is often limited to the hands and feet. In the toes, both the metatarso-phalangeal and the inter-phalangeal joints are involved producing a characteristic square shaped toe. Also characteristic of this type of joint disease are lesions of the nails of which pitting is the most common.

Treatment

Treatments are similar to those discussed for rheumatoid arthritis. The rash produced by the psoriasis may be irritated by footwear and hose and these will need to be carefully chosen to avoid the sensitive areas. Soft leather uppers may help and socks of softer material, for example, cotton rather than synthetic materials, can be more comfortable (see Appendix II). If during treatment the foot has to be heavily bandaged, standard footwear may no longer fit. Sandals with buckles at ankle and toe may provide sufficient adjustment or long-opening footwear (see page 105) may be required.

The pitting of the nails may need the special attention of a chiropodist.

Gout

Of all the joint diseases, gout is the one most dramatically associated with the foot. Historically, paintings and prints of gouty individuals with their foot bandaged and supported on a cushion are almost caricatures (see Fig. 43).

Fig. 43. 'Gouty individual'

Gout most commonly affects the metatarso-phalangeal joint of the big toe but it may also involve other joints in the body. Gout is really a metabolic disease in which there is an abnormally high quantity of uric acid in the blood. This leads to the deposition of uric acid crystals in the fluid lining the joint (synovial fluid) which cause an acute episode of arthritis. These acute episodes produce excruciating pain but this may be relieved and the episode cut short by modern drug treatment. As time goes by, more joints may become involved. Apart from the joint disease, tophi or 'chalk stones' may occur. These consist of deposits of uric acid crystals (urates) and appear on the skin as nodules which may then ulcerate. They are usually found on the outer rim of the ear and may occur also on the toes. Whilst gout (also called 'podagra' which literally means a trap for the feet) is most commonly a primary disease of unknown origin, there are secondary forms occasionally associated with certain drug treatment.

Treatment

In the treatment of gout, footwear must be chosen to suit the symptoms and may need to be wide fitting with soft uppers possibly of felt of plastazote. If the pain is brought on by movement of the toe, a rocker sole which will prevent the big toe joint from bending when walking will be needed (see page 132).

Other joint diseases can cause inflammatory changes in the feet, e.g. Reiter's Disease, but the treatments are similar to those already discussed.

Osteoarthrosis

In contrast to rheumatoid arthritis in which inflammation can be widespread, osteoarthrosis is almost entirely a disease of joints. It is a disease of middle aged and elderly people and the deformities which it produces are cumulative as age advances. In this deasease, destruction of articular cartilage is followed by a deforming process affecting the bone ends. Weight bearing joints are particularly affected and may be very painful.

There are two main types of osteoarthrosis – the primary generalised form and the various secondary forms.

Primary generalised osteoarthrosis is a disease of females in middle and later life. The joint involvement can be symmetrical or asymmetrical but, although the hands may be deformed quite badly in this disease (Heberden's nodes), the only problem likely to occur in the feet will be a stifness in the back of the foot.

Secondary osteoarthrosis is more likely to by asymmetrical and involves particularly the weight-bearing joints (hips and knees) and the shoulder joint. This disease may be secondary to many factors including previous disease or injury to joints, unusual strains because of deformities in joints elsewhere in the legs, or occupational strains and stresses to joints and, probably, stresses produced by long-term obesity. The most common site of secondary osteoarthrosis occurring in the foot is in the big toe. The effect of this is to cause *hallux rigidus* (see page 15).

Another part of the foot which can be affected by osteoarthrosis is the mid tarsal joint. The symptoms of this are pain in the forefoot and a lump on the instep.

Treatment

The treatment for *hallux rigidus* has been discussed on page 15. The pain from osteo-arthrosis affecting the mid-foot can be relieved by wearing wedge-soled shoes which support the painful area. Physiotherapy can also be helpful by mobilising the painful joint. People with degenerative joint disease often find walking easier in the morning and activities should be planned with this in mind.

Disease of the Central Nervous System (Neurological)

Disturbance of the nervous system can affect the body in two ways depending on whether the damaged nerve has a motor or a sensory function. Motor nerve deficits cause muscle weakness and paralysis with or without abnormalities in muscle tone. Tone may increase (hypertonicity or spasticity) making the muscle stiff, or it may decrease (hypotonicity or flaccidity) causing floppiness. As a result of this, there may be a loss of selected movement patterns or disorders of the postural reflex mechanism. Sensory nerve deficits cause disorders in sensation (anaesthesia or paraesthesia) by disrupting the body's awareness and response to impulses on their way to the brain (afferent). This can affect not only skin and joint sensation but also co-ordination and awareness of the body's position in space.

Motor nerves

Whatever the reason for the weakness or paralysis, the symptoms in the foot are similar. The most common of these are foot drop which is associated with difficulty in bending the foot up (dorsiflexion) and in turning it outwards (eversion) (see page 4). This makes walking difficult as the toes drag on the ground and the foot turns in. As a result of the foot drop the posture and control of the rest of the leg and trunk is often affected during standing and walking.

Treatment

Treatment should be directed towards the cause of the problem, for example, spasticity or muscle weakness, which may be in the leg and trunk as well as the foot.

Spasticity can be controlled during treatment by a large number of techniques including ice, weight-bearing on the affected leg and by using movement patterns which cause a reflex inhibition of the spasticity.

Slow passive movement and stretching of the *achilles tendon* should be practised regularly to maintain a full range of movement at the ankle. Nothing should be placed under the spastic foot in bed at night as this may stimulate the extensor pattern of spasticity, but it is advisable to use a cradle to relieve the weight of the bedclothes on the foot.

A variety of adaptations to footwear and appliances can help to maintain a normal walking pattern (see page 123). Fixed foot drop may need surgery.

Sensory nerves

Loss of sensation can occur together with paralysis or be the result of other conditions, for example, diabetes. The danger of not being able to feel one's feet at all are that they can be injured without pain and infections become serious before being noticed. The classic example of this is in people with leprosy. Fortunately, this is a rare condition in this country but people with total paralysis of their legs (paraplegics) or people with spina bifida have the same problem, as do those whose nerves have been affected by some other disease like diabetes. Other problems associated with damage to sensory nerves may be the inability to feel the leg when standing or to know where it is in space when walking. This makes walking very slow and laborious and reduces confidence.

Treatment

Scrupulous attention to footcare is needed (see page 143) and the extra measures suggested for people who have diabetes (see page 145) must be followed. In hemiplegia, sensory deficit can improve and, during the period of recovery, the patient may gain clues about their limb position by, for example, looking in the mirror or by directions given by a therapist or helper. The feedback of this type of information is vital for rehabilitating normal movement. Simple ordinary biofeedback techniques, for example, a heel pressure sensor under the heel in the shoe, can help people to know when their heels are on the ground and so improve their confidence and speed of walking.

Disorders of the blood vessels which can affect the feet

Diseases of blood vessels may endanger the foot either by depriving parts of it of blood supply *(ischaemia)* or by making the tissues particularly susceptible to injury as a result of inflammation of the blood vessels *(vasculitis)*.

Atherosclerosis

Atherosclerosis is a disease of arteries in which fatty deposits (plaques) occur on the inner surface of the wall of the artery, in some cases followed by hardening (calcification) or affording a basis for the formation of blood clots *(thrombi)*. These clots may then block the artery or bits may break off forming emboli which block smaller arteries. Atherosclerosis is said to be a disease of western industrial society and is associated with some of its habits such as diet high in saturated fats, cigarette smoking and lack of exercise. Atherosclerosis may also occur in association with other diseases such as high blood pressure, diabetes and kidney disease.

In a foot, a lack of blood supply *(ischaemia)* secondary to atherosclerosis may appear as pallor and coldness, flaking and thinning of the skin, or thickening of the nails.

At a more severe level, actual tissue death (necrosis or gangrene) occurs. Gangrene is due to total deprivation of blood so it begins at points furthest away from the heart. It may affect only the tip of one or more toes; it may progress to affect the larger part of the front part of the foot. The characteristic changes begin with an area of redness which is rapidly followed by a white or blue appearance and eventually the dead tissue becomes black. If there is infection, the area may be wet and soggy or dry and hard. Ischaemia may be associated with pain, at first during exercise and later at rest, often during the night.

Treatment

At present no specific drugs improve the peripheral circulation in atheroma.

Care of the feet is important to keep the skin healthy and clean (see page 143) and well fitting footwear and hose are essential to prevent any external constriction. Self-treatment of corns and callosites is not recommended as any damage may allow infection to take hold quickly due to the diminished blood supply. Treatment by chiropody is therefore essential. Footwear must be well fitting and have a soft lining, e.g. sheepskin, to minimise the possibility of trauma to the thinned skin.

Gangrene may sometimes by prevented by surgery but once it has occurred it is irreversible. Surgical treatment includes direct arterial surgery involving the use of bypasses with human or synthetic grafts.

Diabetes mellitus

Diabetes is a condition in which there is excess sugar in the blood due to a deficiency of the enzyme insulin which allows the body to metabolise the sugar. Depending on the severity of the disease, it can be managed by carefully controlling carbohydrate intake or by insulin injection. All patients, however, may develop serious complications associated with long-term diabetic disease. Damage to the nerves (neuropathy) and blood vessels (vascular disease) combined with infection are the most serious complications affecting the foot of the person with diabetes. Eyesight may also be impaired making footcare difficult.

Narrowing of the arteries (atherosclerosis) occurs in diabetics more extensively and at a younger age than in non-diabetics. Cold feet and cramps in the legs may be experienced due to this vascular disease.

The most common form of the diabetic neuropathy is a peripheral involvement of the nerves of the lower parts of both legs. Sensory impairment involves gradual loss of all types of sensation. Motor impairment starts with loss of ankle jerks and weakness of the intrinsic muscles follows. Long-standing neuropathy can lead to the development of charcot joints in the foot. These are deformities caused by overgrowth of bone as a result of repeated minor injury to the joints.

Long term problems

The major danger of neuropathy combined with vascular disease with or without infection are neuropathic ulcers. A clear understanding of the cause of these ulcers is important because, left unteated, they can progress to gangrene.

Reasons for the formation of ulcers:

1. loss of sensation of the foot can lead to unrecognised injuries which can become infected and lead to ulcers. These can be caused by foreign bodies (stones in the shoes); damage caused while walking barefoot; badly fitting shoes; burns due to heat sources such as hot water bottles or too hot baths; and burns from chemicals which may be found in some corn removers;

2. another source of injury is pressure on the nailbed caused by shoes rubbing on thickened hypertrophic nails. This leads to an ulcer forming beneath the nail which cannot be felt;

3. loss of sensation in the foot can lead to a heavy, spring-less gait. This extra pressure will quickly lead to the formation of callosities under which a particular type of ulcer can form. Infection in such ulcers can lead to tissue damage which may go unnoticed for some time. The infection may track back to a thinner area of skin where it breaks out on the surface, or the ulcer may only be discovered when the callosity is removed by the chiropodist;

4. deformity can occur due to muscle weakness, for example, if the lumbrical muscles are weak the long toe flexor muscles are unopposed allowing the toes to become curled. This claw-toe deformity, often assisted by badly-fitting footwear, leads to excessive pressure on the metatarso-phalangeal joints (see Fig. 44). Pressure sores, which may progress to ulcers, can develop over the proximal interphalangeal joints and under the metatarsal heads.

Treatment

When ulcers have formed, the dead tissue may need to be removed (debridement) and the ulcers to be cleaned and dressed regularly. Healing of the ulcers may be impaired not only by the factors mentioned above but also if the diabetes itself is not under

adequate control. Conversely, the infection itself may jeopardise
the control of the diabetes leading to a high level of sugar in the
blood (hyperglycaemia). Bedrest is not recommended as this may
further limit the circulation and slow down healing. It is important
therefore to continue walking and special footwear may be needed.

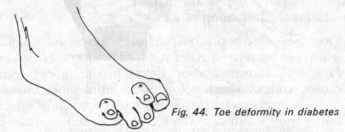

Fig. 44. Toe deformity in diabetes

If a bulky dressing makes it difficult to get shoes on, a low-lacing
shoe (see page 105) allowing for adjustment may be necessary.
When the ulcer is extensive, shoes made out of a soft, moulded
plastic called plastazote may be recommended (see page 112).
When diabetic neuropathy has led to abnormal weight-bearing,
pads (see page 68), padded insoles or specially moulded shoes can
relieve the uneven pressures during standing and walking and
improve full foot function in the already deformed foot.

Surgery to relieve the pressure can only be attempted when the
blood supply is good enough to ensure healing. Removal of the
metatarsal heads to alleviate the pressure or severing of the toe
tendons to relax curly toes might be considered. If the infection has
progressed, amputation may be necessary – the level depending
upon the damage which has occurred.

Fig. 45. Sitting with feet up

Fig. 46. Sitting positions predisposing to pressure sores

Prevention

Diabetics should understand the way in which the disease can affect the feet, how the feet can best be looked after and what should be done about serious problems if they arise. They should understand that the symptoms may be intermittent or come on very gradually and they must be encouraged not to ignore them. Particular attention to footwear is important. Useful leaflets on footcare for diabetic patients are available from the Society of Chiropodists and the British Diabetic Association; the points to watch for are detailed on page 145. Footcare advice should be given as soon as the disease is diagnosed and, if the advice is followed rigorously from the start, many of the factors causing ulcers can be avoided.

SCORING SYSTEM KEY: TOTAL SCORE OF 14 AND BELOW = 'AT RISK'				
A Physical condition	**B** Mental condition	**C** Activity	**D** Mobility	**E** Incontinent
Good 4	Alert 4	Ambulant 4	Full 4	Not 4
Fair 3	Apathetic 3	Walk/Help 3	Slightly limited 3	Occasionally 3
Poor 2	Confused 2	Chairbound 2	Very limited 2	Usually Urine 2
Very bad 1	Stuporous 1	Bedfast 1	Immobile 1	Doubly 1

Fig. 47. Norton's scale

Swelling of the feet and ankles

Swelling of the feet and ankles may occur in many different medical conditions. It may make footcare more difficult or necessitate special shoes.

Soft swelling (pitting oedema) can be the result of abnormal fluid balance in the body. Normally the proportions of fluid in the body cells, the fluid part of the blood and the space between the blood vessels and the body cells (extra cellular space) is very tightly balanced (equilibrium). This balance is governed by the action of chemicals (electrolytes) in the different compartments.

The balance will be upset if:

1. there is a change in the elctrolyte ratio in the compartments brought about by disease either in the liver or kidneys. This type of swelling occurs all over the body;

2. if certain chemicals are released into the extra-cellular spaces as a result of damage to tissue in injury or inflammation. In such a case, the swelling will be seen near to the injury, for example, a sprained ankle;

3. if the pressure in the capilliaries or the blood vessels rises due to the obstruction in the vessels or over-loading of the circulation. In this case, swelling will occur in those parts of the body which hang down (dependant). It can occur as a result of inactivity combined with the prolonged effect of gravity in people who stand immobile or sit for long periods with their feet hanging down, for example, during long journeys by air or while sitting in a wheelchair. Inactivity means that the muscular pump operated by the calf muscle is not being used to help return blood to the heart. This type of swelling may also be due to certain forms of heart disease when the blood returning to the heart is clinically obstructed (congestive cardiac failure).

Swelling of a different sort can occur when the lymphatic system is not working properly. The function of this system is to collect fluid and protein which has leaked out into the extra-cellular space and return it to the blood stream. This type of swelling (lymphoedema) is much firmer to the touch than the other swellings described and can occur anywhere in the body. it is often seen in the leg in association with chronic ulceration or infection of the tissues (cellulitis).

Treatment

Pitting oedema can sometimes be treated by 'water tablets' (diuretics) which affect the fluid balance in the body. Many physiotherapy treatments can help to reduce swelling (see page 74). Those people whose ankles have a tendency to swell can overcome this to a certain extent by careful management of the problem, for example, the beneficial effect of lying down can be enhanced by raising the end of the bed on blocks. Putting shoes on immediately on rising is also a good idea as, later in the day, it may be difficult to ease the feet and ankles, if swollen, into ordinary footwear. Sitting with the feet up for periods during the day is also advisable but sitting with the feet on a stool may not solve the problem (see page 76). The feet must be higher than the hips to allow gravity to help reduce the swelling, and it may be better to lie down for a period with the feet resting on a pillow on the end of the bed or on the arm of a sofa (see Fig. 45).

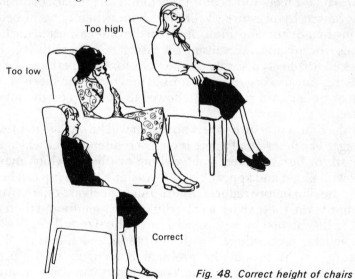

Fig. 48. Correct height of chairs

If the legs are swollen, suitable footwear can be difficult to find, but shuffling along in ill-fitting slippers will mean that the muscular pump in the calf will not be adequately used, and so aggravate the problem. Low-lacing footwear or a fastening which allows adjustment to cope with the fluctuations in the swelling will be needed (see page 105).

Pressure sores

Pressure sores occur when the blood is prevented from circulating through an area of tissue due to unrelieved pressure. Under normal circumstances, the body recognises the dangers of pressure and responds to the discomfort caused by moving. If the sensory nerves are damaged or if immobility is enforced for any reason, for example, by paralysis, this mechanism cannot operate and failure to move can result in a sore. Pressure sores can also be caused by shearing or friction forces. These occur when the skin's response to stretch have been dimished, for example with increasing age. During certain activities, such as moving about in bed, the skin stays in contact with the bed and the shearing effect between the skin and underlying tissue can cause damage to the small blood vessels which may result in a sore. The combination of the shearing effect and pressure often gives rise to sores in people who would not otherwise be thought to be at risk.

Sores on the feet– most commonly found on the back of the heels – are caused by pressure of the heel bone when lying in bed or moving to the sitting position. Sores on the outer aspect of the heels can also occur and are caused by sitting relaxed with legs out-stretched, the heels pressing on the floor for long periods (see Fig. 46). Sores can also occur on the tops of toes when the sheets rest on them or under hard skin if it is allowed to build up on the soles of the feet.

By the time a pressure sore is noticed it will be too late to prevent damage. The first sign of a sore is often a reddened area which may be hard, or be associated with swelling or blisters which may be filled with blood and appear black. Occasionally, a lump can be felt under the skin before redness occurs, but as heels are often covered with hard skin, these signs may be difficult to identify and therefore need to be watched for with special care. The size and depth of the sore will be proportional to the duration and intensity of the pressure, so the sooner the problem is recognised, the better. Unrelieved pressure for as little as two hours can cause a sore in some conditions which may take months to heal.

Healing must occur from the bottom of the sore and cannot start until all the damaged tissues have been removed, possibly by surgery. The healing time will vary according to the general state of health of the patient and on how successfully pressure is relieved from the area. Pressure sores are a serious complication to recovery; they will prevent shoe wear and delay rehabilitation.

Fig. 49. Wedge behind feet to prevent slipping down in bed

Treatment

Complete relief of pressure from the area is the most important factor in the treatment of sores on the feet. The position in which the sore formed must be avoided; for example, if the sores are on the backs of the heels, it will be necessary to lie on the sides and tummy. Sorbo rubber or pillow pads, air or gel cushions or sheepskins may be used to relieve pressure from bony prominences, or if carefully positioned, leave areas such as the heel clear of the mattress.

Further treatment will depend on the severity of the sore; if necessary, dead tissue must be removed and it is important that the area is kept clean while healing takes place. General health is important too. If a person is poorly nourished, healing will be slow, and a high protein diet with vitamins may be advised. Physiotherapy exercises to improve the circulation may also help. Because of the length of time these sores take to disappear, every possible precaution should be taken to prevent them happening.

Prevention

It is most important that the people at risk should be identified.

One method of assessing people at risk is to award a score for different factors (the 'Norton' scale) (see Fig. 47). This is an ideal method for older people but the scale may not be so helpful for younger disabled people who may have a mistakenly high score while still at risk. Particularly at risk are all those confined to bed; all those who cannot move themselves due to paralysis or painful stiff joints; all those on night sedation who will remain immobile at night unless turned by nursing staff; all those with poor blood supply to the feet and/or people with altered sensation in their feet. Any of these factors combined with poor general condition, for example, under-nourishment, will increase the risk significantly.

It must be remembered that pressure sores under the heel can occur when a person is chairbound as well as when confined to bed. For instance, someone with a stroke may sit all day and put a great deal of pressure on the heel. If the weight is taken squarely on the sole of the heel, there is probably little danger as the skin on the sole is designed for taking such pressures, but if, as often happens, the chair is at the wrong height and pressure is taken on the back or sides of the heel, pressure sores can occur. Incorrect chair height can increase pressure on other areas; if it is too low, the knees will be raised so that the pressure on the sacrum and buttocks is increased; if it is too high, the feet will dangle so that the pressure on the backs of the legs is increased (see Fig. 48). People sitting in chairs or wheelchairs for long periods should be taught to lift their legs once every 20 minutes to relieve the pressure and allow the blood to flow back into the area.

Another group at risk consists of those who are constantly sitting up and slipping down in bed. A friction and shearing force occurs from sliding down the bed or from being pulled up again. The slipping can be prevented if the foot of the bed is raised by a couple of inches or if a wedge, for example, a pillow rolled up in a sheet and tucked in either side, is placed in the bottom of the bed so that the feet can rest on this (see Fig. 49). A wedge placed under the knees is harmful; it can increase the risk of blood clotting in the legs (thrombosis) by obstructing the blood vessels to and from the lower leg, and can also put extra weight on the sacrum giving rise to sores there. When helping people to sit up in bed, the heels should not be allowed to drag along the bed. If possible, two people should lift, one on either side, so that the whole person is *lifted* and repositioned. If the person in bed can help by bending their knees and pushing with their feet, this will assist the lift and prevent drag, but if the feet slip, the risk of damage is just as great. If this is likely it is advisable to provide the feet with a non-slip surface, for example a non-slip slipper or inside-out tubipad.

The position of a person in bed should be changed frequently and all pressure areas (for example, areas of redness over the heels) should be checked regularly. The bottom sheet must be kept smooth and dry as wrinkles or crumbs in the bed will increase local pressure and sweat or urine can have a corrosive effect. The weight of the bedclothes can be prevented from pressing on the feet if a tuck is taken in the bedclothes over the feet as the bed is being made or if the person in bed is made to cross his legs while the sheet is being tucked in. This has the effect of tenting the bedclothes so that, when the legs are uncrossed, the bedclothes are slack. Bed cradles are even more effective but, when not available, a tray placed upright in the end of the bed can have a similar effect (see Fig. 50).

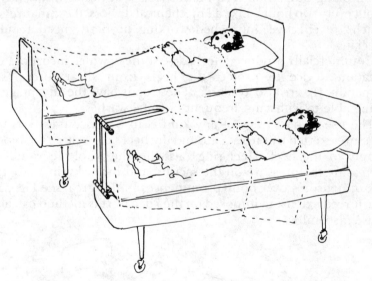

Fig. 50. Ways of elevating bedclothes to keep pressure off the feet

Another form of prevention is to ensure that the pressure points on the body are cushioned. In bed, a 2½cm (1 in) layer of foam placed on the mattress underneath the sheet can give some protection as can specially shaped foam pads placed on the sheet (for example, 'egg box foam' (Lyopad) – see Appendix II). Natural and synthetic sheepskin products in contact with the heels are also beneficial (see Appendix II). Sheepskin bootees ensure that the heels are cushioned at all times but can be very hot to wear and need to be checked regularly to see that circulation is not being constricted by the method of fixing the bootees. Squares of sheepskin are cooler as they allow air to circulate, but these squares tend to move around in the bed. A solution to both these problems is to sew the sheepskin or square of synthetic sheepskin to a draw sheet and put this at the foot of the bed. The drawsheet can be tucked in and so prevent the sheepskin from moving. However, if the patient is mobile he may tuck his feet underneath this drawsheet defeating the object. One way of preventing this from happening is to place a standard drawsheet over the top edge of the first.

Ripple mattresses are another useful aid in the prevention of pressure sores. The cells of these mattresses inflate and deflate alternately to relieve pressure. A person still needs to be turned when being nursed on a ripple mattress but not as frequently – about every two hours. Like all mechanical devices, these mattresses which are effective only when working properly, need regular checking.

Commercially produced heel pads, some of which incorporate a flotation device to protect the heels from shear forces (see Appendix II), are also available. These pads have the advantage of being able to withstand frequent hospital washes.

The use of heel rings of any kind is to be discouraged as the pressure exerted by the ring around the heel can occlude the blood supply to the heel. Heel rings also lift the whole leg and, by increasing the pressure on the sacrum and buttocks, increase the risk of bedsores over bony prominences in this area (see Fig. 51). The forced extension imposed on the knee by this method can also cause discomfort.

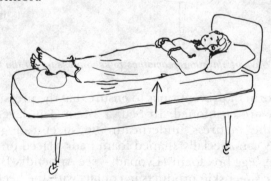

Fig. 51. Effect of a heel ring

If the leg is in a plaster cast, the extra weight which increases the risk of sores on the heels can be counteracted by placing a pillow or pad under the whole leg leaving the heel free. Foam leg gutters are manufactured for this purpose (see Appendix II).

Wearing bedsocks can help to cut down any friction between the heel and the bottom sheet, as can wearing a sock (from toe to below knee) of tubipad (tubular stockinette with foam padding down one side (see Appendix II) as it acts as a sock and a pad, although this 'sock' can be dangerous if too tight. It is available in several sizes, but the fact that it shrinks when washed should be borne in mind when selecting the size initially.

5

Nursing Care

Many people have problems associated with their feet which they do not know how to solve themselves and about which they are too embarrassed to seek professional help. Nurses meet such people during their work and, having gained their confidence, may be able to suggest the best course of action to be taken.

The modern nurse is trained to identify and supply appropriate nursing care for the patient's health problems. This approach, called the nursing process, can be broken down into four stages:

1. assessment of problems and needs;
2. planning and setting goals;
3. implementation of the programme;
4. evaluation of the result.

Whether nursing in hospital or at home, this concept of seeing people as individuals together with **all** the factors which may influence their wellbeing helps nurses to provide such people with the help which, otherwise, they would not receive.

The presence of foot pathology may become apparent in the nurse's initial assessment of the problem and appropriate action can be written into the care plan. Even when no specific history is reported, questions relating to foot care and footwear should always be included, particularly when assessing elderly people, in order to ensure that mobility can be maintained. In the past, an assessment of the feet might have been omitted because it is only recently that the essential importance of maintaining mobility for general health has been fully appreciated.

Mobility can be affected by footcare and footwear problems, for example if a big toenail thickens, becomes difficult to cut and grows until shoes can no longer be put on. Recognition of such a problem and referral to a chiropodist may be all that is needed. However, the situation may be more complicated; for example, some people may be afraid that a visit to a chiropodist or hospital may lead to painful treament or they may be worried about something totally unrelated such as the cost of transport to the hospital or clinic (see Fig. 52). A nurse who knows what services and treatments are available can provide reassurance and guidance.

Fig. 52. Anxiety

Footcare in hospital

Routine care

Detailed observation of the foot should be carried out as part of general hygiene. Feet should also be checked at least once a day and any changes reported to the senior nurse or doctor in charge of the patient.

Particular attention should be paid to:

1. pressure points particularly the heels. Redness of any area is a danger sign (see page 52);

2. areas of hard skin. When non-weightbearing for long periods, the areas of thickened skin react to the removal of the normal pressure of shoes by cracking. This often painful condition can slow rehabilitation and can be relieved by regular application of olive oil or simple lanolin. It can be prevented by wearing normal footwear whenever possible to maintain the usual pressure points;

3. the webbs between the toes. These areas can quickly become infected. Failure to remove all the soap or to dry properly after washing are two factors which can encourage infection. There is also an increased risk of contracting athlete's foot *(tinea pedis)* in hospital due to communal living (see page 24). This risk can be cut down if all surfaces in contact with the feet are carefully cleansed;

4. colour, temperature and sensation to ensure that no vascular changes are occurring, for example formation of clots (deep vein thrombosis – DVT);

5. the condition of nails; regular nail cutting should be arranged.

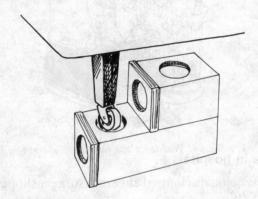

Fig. 53. Blocks to raise the end of the bed

Special footcare

Two categories of patient in hospital may also need special foot care.

One group is the short stay patients with specific foot problems. These patients are likely to have been admitted for surgery to the feet, for example, *hallus valgus* (see page 11). After foot surgery patients will need special care including elevation of the limb for the first 48 hours following the operation to prevent swelling. In some hospitals the practice is to raise the foot of the bed (see Fig. 53); in others, to raise the affected limb on pillows. If an arthrodesis has been performed, the foot will be in a plaster cast until new bone (callus formation) appears on X-ray (approximately four to eight) weeks) following the operation. In other operations, wooden clogs or sandals (see Fig. 54) are used as the standard form of splinting for early rehabilitation. These clogs, which prevent the foot bones from moving while walking, can be uncomfortable at first and may need to be padded under the heel. They are worn until the patient is able to wear his own shoes again. Patients who have had toes arthrodesed may have surgical pins protruding from the ends of their toes. Usually a cork is put on the end of the pin to protect it, as jarring of these pins can cause extreme pain.

Fig. 54. Wooden clogs worn post-operatively

Patients being discharged after foot surgery should be advised to:

1. alternate exercise with periods of rest:
2. sit with their feet raised; sitting with their feet hanging down may lead to swelling of the lower limb (see page 76);
3. raise the bedclothes above the affected foot at night. Bed cradles for this purpose can be obtained from Red Cross loan stores but, for short periods, a cardboard box or tray under the bedclothes (see Fig. 50) is quite sufficient;
4. pay strict attention to hygiene – daily foot bathing ensures observation;
5. consult their doctor should there be any change in the condition of the limb on which the operation was performed, for example, swelling, pain or discharge from the wound;
6. wear only broad-fitting shoes with low heels and firm (non flexible) soles until the foot is completely healed (leather will be more comfortable, see page 88).

Following foot surgery patients should not return to work until advised to do so by their doctor. Some patients may be able to return to work fairly quickly, but foot surgery can be painful and rehabilitation slow, in which case patients should not expect to return to work for two or three months or even longer.

The second group whose feet will need special attention consists of the patients who, for any reason, are in hospital for a long period.

The pressure areas, including the heels, of those in this group (especially if they are immobile for long periods) will need care, (see page 53) or they may need help with toenail cutting. Nurses often shy away from this type of basic foot care due to the risk of damaging the foot of someone with impaired sensation in their feet (parasthesia/anaesthesia), for example, diabetics (see page 46). The initial assessment will have established the presence of diabetes or other neuropathy so chiropodists need only be called to attend to the nails if they present any problems, for example, if they are thickened or there is infection present.

For longer-stay patients who have medical conditions such as those described in Chapter 4, the role of the nurse may be that of a co-ordinator whose general aim is to maintain the mobility of the patient. When assessing the needs and planning the objectives, the nurse should:

1. bear in mind the type and nature of the disease and its effect on the foot (see Chapter 4);

2. provide the medication prescribed and note its effect with appropriate feedback to the medical staff involved (in relation to pain relief and disease activity);

3. ensure the correct level of rest/exercise to relieve pressure on the foot and aviod wasting of muscles;

4. involve therapists, chiropodists, orthotists or other professionals in the total care of the patient;

5. make available adequate footwear – either by arranging to have it brought from home or arranging for footwear to be provided;

6. advise the patient on foot care and footwear and hose, for example, in the case of skin sensitivity;

7. bear in mind the need for psychological support through active periods of serious conditions.

Depending on his or her condition and personal preferences, each patient will require an individual treatment plan. Regular re-assessment of the problems will ensure that the goals are being achieved.

Footcare in the home

A number of nursing specialists who make visits to patients' homes – notably health visitors and district nurses – have a special role to play in foot care and the maintenance of mobility. Nursing care in the community involves two elements. First, the identification of need and the provision of appropriate nursing care for each patient, and, secondly, the identification of possible problems and their prevention.

Perhaps the greatest danger threatening an elderly person living at home is that of increasing immobility. Apart from specific diseases, immobility may be an insidious process which is brought on by a number of factors, for example arthritis, over-weight (obesity), foot pain, lack of motivation to move ('geriatric depression') or inappropriate footwear. A nurse regularly visiting the home will be in an ideal position to observe and deal with these when possible.

Community nurses also have an advantage over their hospital colleagues since they can assess and advise on problems with full knowledge of the home environment.

Having assessed the problem, the community nurse must decide on the best way of implementing the plan. Implementation may include any of the following:

1. liaison with the general practitioner as the conditions change or referral to domiciliary physiotherapy or occupational therapy as required;

2. referral to the local chiropody clinic or domiciliary service for assessment, mentioning the person's social situation particularly if they are without relatives or friends;

3. liaison with the social services department over the provision of aids where necessary, for example, a hand-rail beside the front door steps;

4. advice to the patient on foot care and footwear both to decrease foot pain and promote mobility, for example, suggesting house shoes instead of loose slippers (see page 103);

5. further advice to the patient on ways of preventing slipping and tripping, for example, avoiding loose rugs on lino floors (see page 164);

6. discussion of problems with relatives, advising them on simple ways in which they can help with footcare at home, for example, washing feet or hosiery, toe nail cutting or by providing transport to services;

7. advice on danger signs to look for, for example, changes in colour of the foot or leg (see page 146).

6

Chiropody

Chiropodists work to maintain foot health: this involves the diagnosis and treatment of pathological foot conditions together with prevention of potential problems.

Chiropody treatments may include modification of existing footwear or advice about the correct type of footwear or hose that should be worn to prevent or halt the progression of deformity; padding is used to take the pressure off, or to cushion, painful areas and permanent appliances are made to perform the same functions or to increase foot function; management of nail conditions by trimming, drilling, bracing or removing the nail is another part of a chiropodist's work as is the cutting of corns and callosities, treatment of *verruca* and care of ulcers. Physical therapies can also be used, for example, ultrasound (see page 75).

Chiropodists see a high proportion of elderly people with foot problems and therefore are often instrumental in helping to maintain their mobility. For example, patients with rheumatoid arthritis (see page 37) can be kept on their feet if their skin lesions are treated and if soft padding is incorporated into an orthosis. In some cases, this can prevent patients from becoming housebound. The monitoring of the skin condition of the feet of people with diabetes (see page 46) can prevent serious ulceration which may otherwise involve long periods in hospital.

Biomechanics

Many foot pathologies are caused by some minor abnormality in the function of the joints or a mechanical problem affecting soft tissues. A biomechanical assessment will determine how well

65

certain key joints and muscles are functioning and many chiropodists include this in their initial evaluation of the problem. Treatment can then be aimed at restoring full function and thereby curing the problem. This is done by making an appliance to maintain active foot movement (see page 70).

Nail treatments

Most adults manage to cut their own toenails but this can be a problem for elderly or disabled people who may have difficulty bending down, have impaired sight or limited function in their hands.

Simple nail cutting does not need the attention of a chiropodist though it is important to check that there is no underlying pathology present. If the nails are uncomplicated, nail care can be carried out by a footcare assistant if one is employed at the clinic or by a friend, relative or health care personnel. Some voluntary organisations, such as the British Red Cross and Age Concern, arrange sessions for simple pedicure.

Any deformity or infection of the nail needs chiropody treatment. Excessive thickening (see page 22) may be another reason why people cannot cut their own toenails. This thickening can easily be reduced if a chiropodist uses an electric drill with a diamond or ruby burr over the nail.

Treatment of ingrowing toenails may entail the removal of the section or splinter of the nail causing the condition followed by careful management of infection if present. If the condition is due to constant pressure on the nail from tight footwear, the nail may have become permanently curved and the condition is likely to recur. In these cases, the chiropodist removes part of the growing section of the nail (matrix) under anaesthesia leaving the nail narrower and able to grow straight again.

Some deformed nails, for example involuted nails (see page 20), may need straightening by means of a brace (similar to dental bracing). This treatment, almost universally confined to young people, involves hooking specially shaped stainless steel wire under the incurved edges of the nail to encourage it to grow straight (see Fig. 55). If this treatment is not successful, it may be necessary to remove part, or all, of the nail.

Fungal infections of the nail are common in elderly people particularly those who live in institutions where cross-infection can occur. These infections do not usually cause pain or discomfort though pain may occur if the surrounding skin becomes infected. A diagnosis is made after the cells have been cultured from a biopsy (microscopic examination of infected cells). Effective treatment of fungal infections of the nail plate takes a long time as treatment has to continue until the nail plate has grown out completely. A course of drug treatment from a doctor may also be needed.

If the condition is not causing any discomfort, the infection may not be treated actively but simply observed from time to time to ensure that it is not spreading to the surrounding skin.

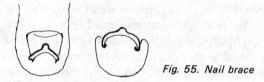

Fig. 55. Nail brace

Skin treatments

Skin lesions, for example corns and callosities, can be very painful and can limit mobility at any age. If they occur in elderly people whose mobility is already reduced, for example by osteo-arthritis, the further reduction in mobility can, in some cases, force the individual to remain housebound.

The use of a scalpel to remove thickened skin and application of padding can relieve the pain from these lesions but the main problem for the chiropodist is to prevent them recurring. Corns are caused by pressure over bony prominences and callosities by friction and shearing stresses (see page 25), and while these forces persist the lesions will recur however often they are removed. Diagnosis of the cause of the lesion is therefore important. Once it has been isolated, treatment aimed at preventing the recurrence of the lesion can be started. A change in style of footwear is the most common remedy as many styles of shoe allow some movement of the foot within the shoe at each step. This friction force, combined with pressure as the foot pushes against the front and sides of badly shaped shoes, can be removed if shoes with fastenings that hold the foot back in the shoe are worn. An appliance to remove the pressure may have to be fitted to ensure the long term relief of painful corns and callosities (see page 70).

Infections of the skin need active treatment to stop them spreading. Warts of the foot *(verrucae),* one of the most common foot infections, are treated by chiropodists in several ways. All treatments involve destroying the skin affected by the virus and a small margin of unaffected skin. Two methods involve burning away the affected skin. The use of caustic chemicals to do this involves several treatments before the *verruca* is completely removed. (Self treatment is not recommended, as unless it is carefully carried out, areas of healthy skin can be destroyed). Electro-surgery performed under local anaesthesia may need only one treatment. A very high frequency current, concentrated at the tip of an electrode, generates intense heat which causes the contents of the affected cells to coagulate, destroying the verruca.

Another method uses intense cold (cryosurgery) to destroy a small section of skin; the cell's contents expand on freezing causing the cell membrane to rupture. This treatment, which can be painful as a blister forms quickly, should be completed in one visit. Care of the wound to prevent it becoming infected is most important after all these treatments.

Ulceration on the foot is another common problem. A variety of conditions can cause ulcers to form on the foot, for example rheumatoid arthritis (see page 39) or diabetes (see page 47) or occasionally the home treatment of callosities can also cause ulceration. Since the blood must be allowed to circulate freely through the area if healing is to take place, it is important to prevent any pressure which may impede the circulation. A tight bandage or simply the weight of a limb pressing down on an area during a long period sitting still could cause pressure (see pressure sores, page 52). Padding may need to be applied around the site of the lesion to take the weight off the affected area while it is healing. Keeping the patient on his feet can be difficult during the treatment of lesions as the type of padding used is often too bulky to fit into standard footwear. In this case, some sort of temporary footwear (see page 118) will be necessary.

Padding

The purpose of chiropody padding is to redistribute pressure or to cushion a specific area. The weight of the body is normally distributed evenly between the ball of the foot and the heel and both these areas are covered by a fatty layer to help to distribute the pressure (see page 6). In elderly people and those with certain systemic conditions, for example rheumatoid arthritis (see page 38), this padding may become thin over the fore part of the foot allowing weight to be taken by individual metatarsal heads. This extra weight increases the pressure on the skin over the bone and leads to the formation of painful corns and callosities. Chiropody pads are designed to take over the function of the natural padding, either by cushioning the whole area or by taking weight from the pressure point. Cushioning involves covering the whole area with soft material (see Fig. 56) – the thickness and density of the material being varied to suit the patient. Weight is taken from the pressure point by circling the area with a material such as adhesive felt (chiropody felt) so that the pad comes into contact with the ground first and not the pressure point (see Fig. 57). If this type of pad is used for a long time, the tissues may drop down into the centre of the pad. To guard against this, pressure can be relieved if the whole area is covered with a pad made of materials of different densities. Soft materials under the pressure point and harder ones around it achieve a more even distribution of pressure.

Fig. 56. Pad cushioning metatarsal heads

The same principle is applied in padding other areas, for example felt may be cut to fit around a corn or a crescent pad may be placed behind the bunion in *hallux valgus* (see Fig. 58). Adhesive materials applied over long periods can make foot hygiene difficult and the skin needs to be checked regularly for signs of allergy. Once an effective shape of pad has been found, this can be used as a pattern for a more permanent appliance.

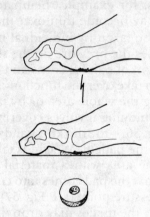

Fig. 57. Pad encircling an area so that the pad comes into contact with the ground first

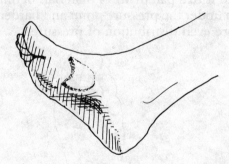

Fig. 58. Crescent pad behind the bunion in hallux valgus

Orthoses (appliances)

Orthoses are either removable, fitting on to the foot or into a shoe, or are incorporated permanently into the shoe as a modification. They have the same effect as padding but have the advantage that they do not have to be stuck on and can also be used to re-align the foot into a good functional position (see page 126, Chapter 9).

Orthoses which fit onto the foot are not suitable for people who have difficulty in reaching their feet as they may be unable to position them accurately. These orthoses, which can be made of a variety of substances depending on the density of padding required and are usually covered in leather, are attached to the foot with a loop around a toe or an elastic strap around the forefoot (see Fig. 59).

Removable orthoses can also be moulded out of latex rubber. One example, a *hallux valgus* shield, provides a close fitting sleeve which protects the tender joint. To increase the protection over the bunion, a 'false' bursa can be created, by injecting liquid silicone into the shield over the bunion to act as an extra cushion and reduce the friction.

Silicone rubber can also be used to make orthoses for the toes. These may be used to straighten toes which have a tendency to become hammer toes (see page 18) or to keep all toes in a functional position for walking (see Fig. 60). These orthoses fit between the toes.

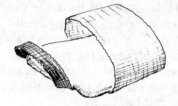

Fig. 59. A removable orthosis/appliance

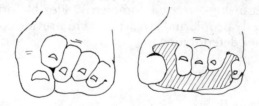

Fig. 60. Silicone rubber appliance to fit between the toes

Orthoses which fit into the shoe are made of a variety of materials depending on the required density. They are usually formed on a thin leather covered insole cut to fit the inside of the shoe, to ensure that the orthosis will be in the correct position at all times. This is important as the padding on the insole is designed to relieve pressure from a certain area. If it is allowed to move, it may increase the pressure and make the condition worse. It is for this reason that loose removable insoles cannot be fitted into sandals as the upper straps cannot control the position of the insole. If necessary an insole can be fixed into a shoe or sandal to prevent movement.

Slip-on court shoes present similar problems as, although the insole can be anchored inside the shoe, the foot cannot be so anchored (see page 99). Usually, therefore, orthoses are made only to fit into shoes which have some form of fastening, either a lace or a bar to hold the foot back into the shoe. The shoe should also have a fairly low heel to keep the weight distribution balanced (see page 100). Whenever possible, chiropody insoles are made to fit into the existing footwear and unless bulky, will fit into standard depth footwear.

One way of identifying where the pressure points on the sole of the foot occur is by taking a footprint in the shoe (pedograph). This involves fitting a temporary cardboard insole into the shoe. The pressure points on the foot are marked with wax crayon or other material which will rub off on the insole and the shoe applied., Taking a few steps with this in the shoe leaves an accurate map of the pressure points on the card, so that insoles with soft padding in these marked areas can be made.

Insoles are also produced by taking a cast of the foot as described in Chapter 9.

When the foot is not functioning correctly (see page 65), a rigid or flexible corrective insole (orthosis) may be made. The rigid type is made more commonly for young people or athletes when the malfunction can be corrected completely. Flexible orthoses are made for elderly people and are designed to provide comfort and prevent further deterioration.

Advice

Most chiropody treatments will include some form of advice about the best way to look after the feet, as well as advice about the most suitable type of footwear for the particular condition.

The advice might include details on general footcare, for example how to apply a lanolin and paraffin preparation after washing in cases where there is dry skin (anhydrosis); how to maintain immaculate personal hygiene to prevent spreading of fungus infections; specific footwear advice, for example a person with *hallux valgus* would be advised to wear laced shoes with a straight inside border.

Following the advice which has been given between treatments will help a great deal.

There are many areas in which chiropody can help a patient with foot problems. It is also clear that the earlier chiropody is started, the simpler the remedy is likely to be. Many people whose foot problems can be treated remain unhelped because of their lack of knowledge or because they assume that their aches and pains are part of getting old. While it is hoped that the chiropody service will one day be able to provide a screening service to isolate and treat such people, no such service exists at the present time except in isolated areas where a school service exists. Anyone with a foot problem should therefore be directed to the nearest chiropody clinic or state registered chiropodist.

Further details on chiropody services and those patients eligible for treatment from the National Health Service are given in the Appendix (see page 170).

7

Physiotherapy

It is not unusual for someone to be referred to a physiotherapist specifically for treatment of the foot, for example, sprained ankle or *achilles tendonitis,* and many people who have physiotherapy are likely to have foot problems which may hinder their rehabilitation. Healthy feet are essential for effective rehabilitation so there is much to gain by ensuring that the feet and footwear of patients are kept in good condition.

The help that physiotherapists can give to their patients falls into two categories – actual treatment of the foot, for example the control of swelling following ankle injury, or other help which can be broadly grouped under the heading of the maintenance of mobility.

Treatments

Normally, the treatments discussed would be given in a physiotherapy department following referral from a doctor. None of these are exclusively for the feet but all can be used to relieve one or more symptoms which may occur in the foot, for example pain or stiffness. A detailed assessment of the patient's problems will normally precede any form of treatment.

Reduction of swelling in the feet and ankles

Swelling can occur in the foot for a number of reasons. The mechanisms which upset fluid balance in the area and allow swelling to occur (described in Chapter 4) will dictate the type of treatment which may be used to relieve it.

Injury to a ligament (e.g. a sprained ankle) causes a release of chemicals into the blood stream, which, in turn causes swelling to the area and can be helped by several methods.

Cold treatment in any form is an effective form of first aid for recent injury as it can help to prevent swelling occurring. Examples of this would be an ice pack (crushed ice wrapped in a damp towel), a packet of frozen peas (also wrapped in a damp towel) or immersing the injured foot in cold water or holding it under running cold water.

Application of cold to the site of the injury leads to a decrease in blood flow to the area and so helps to reduce the amount of swelling being produced. Cold treatment can also be useful in the later stages of swelling due to injury but is often used in combination with other therapies, for example, ultrasound and electrical stimulation.

Ultrasound is a technique which uses sound waves at a higher frequency than can be heard by the human ear to produce a number of beneficial effects (thermal and non-thermal). These sound waves cause minute vibrations within the tissues themselves which has the effect of hastening the removal of fluid from the damaged area.

For established swelling, techniques which increase the blood supply can also be beneficial (see page 77). This helps in three ways — first, more blood flowing through the area enables more fluid to be absorbed so that the swelling is reduced. Secondly, the increased blood flow to the area helps to carry away the injury 'chemicals' produced by the initial damage. This helps to restore the fluid balance and prevent further swelling in the area. Thirdly, increased blood flow increases the supply of stimulatory factors and raw materials needed to begin repair of the damage.

The type of swelling caused by overloading of the circulation (see page 50) can be helped by intermittent compression therapy. One form of this treatment is the use of air pressure from a small pump to distend a double-walled, nylon, full-length boot every few seconds (flowtron and flowpulse). This alternating pressure imitates the pumping action of the calf muscle during walking which helps to reduce the swelling. These treatments should always be followed by up and down ankle movements (dorsiflexion exercises) (see Fig. 61).

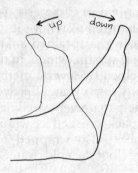

Fig. 61. Dorsiflexion exercise

The swelling collects in the feet and ankles because they hang down for most of the day and gravity is constantly working against the pumping action of the heart. The effect that gravity has on the capillary circulation can be counteracted by regular elevation of the leg. For elevation to be effective the feet must be higher than the hips (see Fig. 62). Even if the feet are raised on a stool or the sofa they are still probably lower than any other part of the body and therefore still the hardest part to pump blood back from. Lying with the feet resting up on the end of the bed or the arm of the sofa are

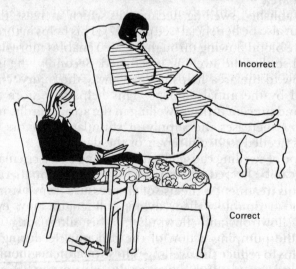

Fig. 62. Elevation of the leg — feet on a stool (correct and incorrect)

even better positions to relieve swelling. Elevation of the leg can be even more effective if combined with up and down movements of the foot as the muscular action helps to pump the blood up the leg (see Fig. 61). Lying on a bed or the floor with the feet resting against a wall so that they can be 'walked up' the wall is another activity that can be performed to help to relieve swelling.

Relief of pain in the foot

A number of conditions can cause pain in the foot. Those which can be particularly helped by physiotherapy are tendon or soft tissue injury, for example, *achilles tendonitis* or *plantar fascitis,* and arthritic pain, for example, *hallux rigidis.*

One treatment which can relieve painful joints is manipulation. There are several types of manipulation (the treatment of stiff or painful joints by passive movements). The types used by physiotherapists are known as mobilisations to differentiate them from more forcible manipulative techniques. Applying repetitive passive movements within the pain-free range has a calming effect on the nerve endings in the joint. Special training is needed in this form of treatment as inexperienced handling of a painful joint may aggravate the pain instead of relieving it.

Often the main difficulty in mobilising painful joints is the pain itself. If this can be removed even temporarily, active movement or exercises to improve muscle power may be beneficial. In such cases, the application of an ice pack, ultrasound or low frequency current may reduce the pain sufficiently for the exercises to be performed.

Increase of the blood supply

Techniques which increase the blood supply to an area of the body are useful in several ways. For example, an increase in blood supply to the area of an established swelling can help to remove the injury chemicals and bring more oxygen and infection-fighting cells (leucocytes) to the area which may accelerate the healing process.

One way in which the blood supply can be augmented is to increase the temperature of the area; this dilates the blood vessels (vasodilation). Superficial heat treatments like infra-red will only heat the surface area and, if the tissue to be treated is deeper than the skin, another method must be used. The deep heating required can be provided by ultrasound – a method by which the tissues can be selectively heated. Heat is produced when sound waves are absorbed by the tissues – certain tissues (those with high protein) – like collagenous scar tissue or the bone covering *(periostium)* – are heated more readily than tissues containing little protein, e.g. fat (adipose tissue), so the deep structures can be treated without overheating the surface. Furthermore, the depth of penetration is related to the ultrasonic frequency: the lower the frequency the deeper the penetration. Deep structures can also be heated by short wave diathermy but this method is not as selective as ultrasound as most body tissues (except fat) are good conductors of the currents produced.

The blood supply to an area can also be increased by stimulation using a low frequency current (interferential). The application of low frequency currents to the body has been shown to produce beneficial effects which vary according to the frequency of the current used. It has a direct effect on the nerves which act on the blood vessels. This causes dilation of the blood vessels (vasodilation) to the area supplied by the nerves stimulated.

Increase of range of movement of joints

Pain or stiffness can occur in any one of the many joints in the foot. Gentle repetitive movements (manipulation) within the painfree range can be used to increase the range of movement in stiff joints. These movements reproduce passively the normal active joint range and also the accessory movements which, although essential for the joint's normal function, are not performed actively.

Manipulation is rarely given in isolation; it may be combined with treatment such as ultrasound and footwear advice and walking training (gait re-education) should always be given to prevent the likelihood of a recurrence.

Ultrasound can also help to increase the range of movement in stiff joints. It is particularly effective for stiffness following injury or inflammation, possibly because of the heat produced by the ultrasound. When fibrous tissue is heated the collagen it is not rich in becomes more elastic. Joints will also be able to move more freely once pain or swelling has been relieved (see page 77 and 74).

Stimulation of growth of new tissue

Ultrasound can increase the rate of tissue repair and this can be useful following injury, or in the case of gravitational (varicose) ulcers or pressure (trophic) ulcers. This is attributed to the non-thermal effects of ultrasound.

Re-education

Of the many methods of re-education of muscles available, two are of particular use in the region of the foot. The first is helpful in cases of foot strain or feet which have become stiff due to disuse, for example following immobilisation in a plaster cast. This treatment consists of another form of electrical stimulation. Stimulation with a low frequency current (faradism) can cause muscles to contract. Such stimulation can be applied to the small muscles of the foot (intrinsic muscle) to help to 'remind' the muscle how to work. The stimulation is always combined with active exercises (see Fig. 63) and, as soon as the movement can be done independently, it can be discontinued.

The other form of rehabilitation of particular relevance to the foot is the retraining of balance. The messages sent to the brain by special nerve endings (proprioceptors) situated in tendons, joints and muscles govern the sense of movement and position of the limbs. If these nerve endings are damaged by injury, balance is disturbed and the likelihood of further injury is increased. Exercise performed while standing on a balance board is one of the most effective methods used to retrain the ability to balance (see Fig. 64, page 81). A balance board is flat with a rounded base on which standing is precarious until some sense of balance is achieved. Exercises of this sort can be graded to suit ability, the ultimate test being the ability to balance on one leg on the board with ease.

Physiotherapists can use many other techniques, but discussion has been confined to those most likely to be used on or around the feet for a specific foot problem or the maintenance of mobility.

Maintenance of mobility

In the course of their work, physiotherapists will see many patients who, for one reason or another, have difficulty in walking – for example, people with rheumatoid arthritis or those who have had strokes. By and large, these patients will be attending physiotherapy departments and treatments will be directed towards the individual problems experienced. This may include footwear advice, provision of aids or adaptations, hydrotherapy, co-ordination exercises for the legs or walking training. Careful assessment, will precede any treatments which can then be directed at the cause of the problem, for example, the relaxation of spasticity when this is making walking difficult.

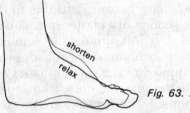

Fig. 63. Foot arching exercise

Elderly people who, due to specific disease or general debility, have become inactive will also need help. The dangers of inactivity in elderly people are far greater than they would be for younger people experiencing similar problems. Anyone who has spent a week in bed will know how weak he or she feels on getting up again. Usually this weak feeling passes off as normal activity is resumed but in older people, this is not the case. Weakness develops during shorter periods of inactivity and getting back to normal takes far longer. For this reason, periods in bed should be kept as short as possible and physiotherapists, working in conjunction with the nursing staff and other therapists, can help by encouraging purposeful activity and helping elderly patients to be up for at least part of the day so that function and morale can be maintained.

The longer elderly people are allowed to remain in bed, the greater the risk of other complications occurring, all of which are likely to increase the period spent in bed. One example of this is pressure sores (see page 52). These can form in a matter of hours and take many months to heal thus further hindering the resumption of activity.

Long periods in bed can also lead to stiffening of the ankles in the downward pointing position. This is caused by the continuous pressure of bedclothes and is particularly likely to happen if the sheets are tucked in tightly. Once the ankles have become stiff, standing will be made very difficult as the feet will not move easily to a right-angle and walking will have to be delayed until this activity is regained. Placing a bed cradle in the bed to keep the weight of the bedclothes off the feet and allow free movement of the legs and feet is one way of preventing this problem from occurring, others are discussed on page 55.

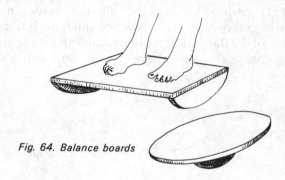

Fig. 64. Balance boards

Another problem associated with bed rest and immobility is clotting of the blood in the legs (deep vein thrombosis). Patients with heart disease and those recovering from operations are particularly at risk and will need some form of active leg exercises during each day to diminish the risk of stagnation of the blood in the calf *(venous stasis)*.

Thinning of the bones (osteoporosis) is yet another danger resulting from long periods of inactivity. It occurs more often in elderly women than in elderly men and will increase the risk of breaking bones (fractures) following accidents.

Whenever it is possible, therefore, the risk of these complications must be reduced by encouraging elderly people to move about in bed and get up for periods each day. This will be the aim of all hospital staff concerned with the care of the patient, but the physiotherapist will be particularly involved and will be responsible for the provision of walking aids if necessary, or temporary footwear (see page 118). Temporary footwear will be necessary if the patient has no suitable shoes or has the foot bandaged making the wearing of normal shoes impossible. In such a case, a non-slip surface for taking a few steps in the ward can be provided by using inside-out tubipad with the foam layer under the sole of the foot.

It can be seen that physiotherapists have a large part to play in the 'maintenance of mobility' of elderly people admitted to hospital. Their role in the community is similar although the dangers of immobility may be less clearly defined, for example a person having difficulty walking as far as the lavatory may become incontinent if he becomes unable to reach it quickly enough. Provision of a walking aid may be all that is necessary to prevent the onset of incontinence in such a patient and the loss of self-esteem involved. It is impossible to list all the ways in which physiotherapists can help in these types of situation but it is clear that knowledge of the dangers and discussion with those concerned with the patients' care and support will diminish the risks considerably.

8

Footwear

Shoes have been worn for centuries sometimes more as a status symbol and a fashion article than as a protection for the foot; this is still true today (see Fig. 65). Fashions come and go in cycles, the same features occurring again and again. Despite the effect fashion has on footwear, the ways in which shoes are made and the materials used in their construction can have a bearing on comfort and, most importantly, on foot health. For this reason a section on the construction of footwear has been included.

Construction of shoes

Shoes were traditionally made by moulding leather on to a wooden foot-shaped model called a last. Modern technology has brought many new materials to the footwear industry and most of the processes involved in making shoes have been mechanised over the years. Although machinery is now used to help cut, shape and bottom the shoes, a high degree of skill is still required.

Lasts

The shape and dimensions of a last, which are highly dependent on fashion, will dictate the fit and, to some extent, the ultimate durability of the shoe made on it. In design, the type of footwear for which the last was intended and the materials out of which it will be made must be borne in mind.

Lasts are **not** perfect images of the feet – they are shaped to allow for changes in the shape of the foot during walking. Toe spring, for example, is incorporated into most lasts to help compensate for the stiffness of the footwear (see Fig. 66). The more rigid the soling material, the greater the toe spring needed.

Fig. 65. Fashion – 'status symbol and fashion article'

Lasts are designed to incorporate fashion features, for example heel height or toe shape. A last for a high-heeled shoe will be significantly shorter than the length of the foot it is designed for, or a last may be made longer to accommodate a shallow pointed toe. (The part of the last which projects beyond the point of the toe is called the recede, see Fig. 67.)

The constant changes in the shape of lasts are dictated by fashion trends – lasts for fashion shoes may be used for only one season, while lasts for less fashionable footwear (slightly altered each season to take account of changes in style) may be used for a much longer period. People who find it difficult to find shoes to fit should choose these less fashionable shoes and take a note of the shoe manufacturer and the last number (usually found on the shoe box, or occasionally, inside the shoe) when they buy new shoes; if they fit

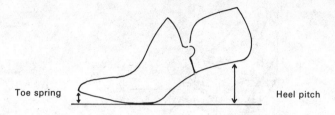

Toe spring   Heel pitch

Fig. 66. A last showing toe spring

well, further pairs of shoes of a similar standard of fit can be identified in this way providing the last is still in use.

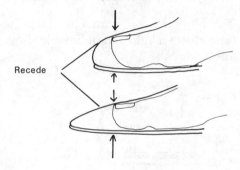

Recede

Fig. 67. Recede

Construction methods

Two of the most important operations in shoe making are lasting and bottoming. In lasting, the upper is shaped to the last and attached to the insole; in bottoming, the sole is attached to the upper. The many different shoe constructions are usually named after the bottoming method used – cementing or moulding, for example. The way in which a shoe is constructed will influence its price, quality, usefulness, style and performance. The most common methods of construction are listed below.

1. *A Goodyear welt* (see Fig. 68) – the sole is firmly stitched to the upper by means of a thin strip of leather called a welt. A sturdy insole is sandwiched between the upper and the sole. The footwear produced by this method can be less flexible than that produced by some other constructions. It is usually used in high quality men's and women's walking shoes.

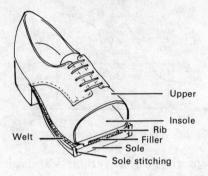

Fig. 68. Goodyear welt construction cross-section

2. *Cementing* (see Fig. 69) – the sole is attached by adhesives. This method, which produces a lightweight flexible shoe, is used for casual and fashion shoes.

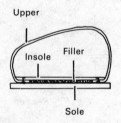

Fig. 69. Cement construction cross-section

3. *Veldshoen (stitched down) method* (see Fig. 70) – the edge of the upper is flanged outwards away from the last before being stitched down on to the sole (lasted out). The slightly larger sole areas of shoes made in this way can help to increase the stability of those with impaired balance. This construction is used for children's sandals, some slippers, lightweight shoes and casual footwear.

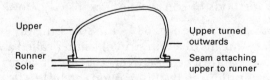

Fig. 70. Veldshoen cross-section

4. *Moulded method* – vulcanising (converting uncured rubber into a stable compound by chemical process) or injection moulding (injecting liquid soling into a mould containing the upper on its last (see Fig. 71)). By these methods, the upper is incorporated permanently into the sole.

5. *Moccasins* – the upper is placed under the last and extends up and round to form the quarters and vamp. The upper is usually completed by stitching in an apron. Soles are applied directly to the upper. This construction is used for lightweight casual shoes and slippers.

While the type of construction and the soling material affect the performance and, to some extent, the comfort of the shoe, other factors such as the last shape and the upper materials are more important to its fit and comfort.

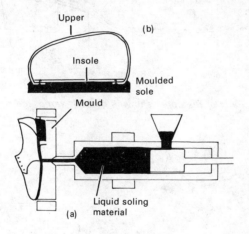

Fig. 71. Moulded construction (method and cross-section)

Uppers

The upper of the shoe protects the foot from cold, damp and dirt.

The part of the upper that covers the back of the foot and heel is called the quarter (see Fig. 72). This section is usually reinforced round the heel by a stiffener (the counter). The forefoot is covered by the vamp which may have a decorative punching or stitching to add to the style. Sometimes a decorative toe cap is added as in a brogue style of shoe. The inside of the toe of the shoe is usually reinforced by a toe puff to maintain its shape.

Two designs of lacing are common. The Gibson (in shoes) and the Derby (in boots) have a wide opening created by stitching the front edge of the quarters over the vamp. They usually have two or three eyelets (see Fig. 73). The Oxford has a narrow V-shaped opening with the front edge of the quarters stitched under the vamp. It usually has four or five eyelets (see Fig. 74).

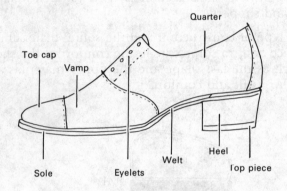

Fig. 72. Parts of the upper showing quarter, vamp, toe cap and toe puff

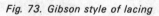

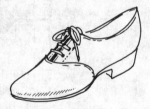

Fig. 73. Gibson style of lacing   Fig. 74. Oxford style of lacing

Upper materials

Leather, always considered to be the best material for making shoe uppers, has certain advantages over synthetic materials. Leather uppers are permeable and absorbent – allowing moisture from perspiration to escape from the foot (breathability); leather uppers will stretch in wear and will permanently mould to (or be stretched to fit over) slight prominences on the foot (see page 135). Uppers made of woven strips of leather conform particularly well but should not be worn over very awkwardly shaped toes as the edges of the strips may rub the skin causing sores.

Shoes made of synthetic upper materials are usually cheaper than those made of leather, and can be as good provided they fit well in the first instance. Some (the poromerics) are also permeable. Unlike leather, synthetic materials will not stretch permanently with wear; they are elastic, and may stretch slightly while being worn but will return to their original shape when taken off. Therefore, shoes made of such materials must fit well when bought. In addition, shoe uppers made of some synthetic materials tend to form one deep crease with wear instead of the many tiny creases found in leather uppers. This problem is unlikely to occur if the shoe fits well but may cause discomfort if the shoe is larger than necessary.

Soft uppers can also be made of fabrics, and shoes made of corduroy can be very comfortable providing they are well constructed.

Linings

Linings are included in the quarters and vamps of many shoes to increase their comfort and durability. Synthetic materials are often used in place of soft leather.

Unless the lining material has the same properties as leather, i.e. that it can be moulded and has the ability to breathe (see page 88), the benefits of having leather uppers will be counteracted. If synthetic linings are restricted to the back part of the shoe (quarters) the loss may not be noticeable, but if such a lining extends to the forepart of the shoe (vamp) the upper will be prevented from moulding to the shape of the foot and perspiration may build up making the foot hot and damp.

Soles and heels

In a traditional shoe, soles and heels are separate and are nailed and stuck or sewn on individually. Many modern shoes have pre-moulded sole and heel units which are attached to the lasted upper with adhesives. Repair to this type of unit is possible but the whole unit may need to be replaced. Moulded soles (see page 87) are very hard wearing but are more difficult to repair as the sole cannot be easily removed without damaging the upper.

Sole materials

It is generally accepted now that synthetic materials are more suitable for the soles of shoes than leather. Not only are they waterproof but many are more durable (and therefore more economical), more flexible, lighter and provide the foot with better insulation from the ground.

Durability, flexibility and lightness of footwear are, to some extent, governed by the sole material, but, as has been seen already, these features also depend on the method of construction. It is therefore not possible to give accurate guidelines regarding these characteristics. In general, a thicker sole will be heavier and more durable and less flexible than thinner soles made of the same material.

Some elderly people are under the impression that a more flexible sole will relieve pain in the sole of their foot, but it may aggravate the problem.

Slip properties

The slip property of a sole is another factor to consider though this will differ considerably on different surfaces and in different conditions. Most people will want the best possible resistance to slip to prevent falls, but some, such as those with Parkinson's Disease, may prefer less friction. In general, cellular materials have a higher resistance to slipping than the same material in solid form and softer materials have a higher resistance than harder materials. When a high degree of slip resistance is required, a distinctive sole pattern with well defined ridges will be most suitable.

Intermediate parts

Between the upper and the sole are several important layers (see Fig. 75).

1. *The insock* – this forms a lining for the bottom of the shoe. It may cover the entire length of the shoe, three-quarters of the length or just the heel section. Insocks are made of leather or

paper/fabric coated with PVC. Leather insocks may be more comfortable as they will absorb perspiration.

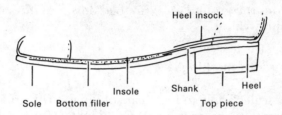

Fig. 75. Intermediate parts showing insock, shank, and insole

2. *The shank* – this is a strip of metal, wood or synthetic material which supports the waist of the shoe and the arch of the foot. Rigid shanks will be most comfortable for those who do a great deal of standing or walking. A wedge sole (one without a separate heel) will have the same effect. Standing for long periods in a shoe with a flexible shank may lead to foot strain. The rigidity of the shank can be tested by pressing down on the middle of the inside of the shoe on a flat surface. A flexible shoe will yield under this pressure (see Fig. 76).

3. *The insole* – this is the layer between the insock and the sole. Insoles are usually made in two parts which are stuck together. The fore part of the insole needs to be flexible as this is where the shoe bends to accommodate the joints between the toes and the metatarsals. This part of the insole is usually made of leather board (leather fibres bonded with rubber) and will mould slightly to the shape of the foot with wear. The back part of the insole needs to be more rigid; it is made of stronger materials and is reinforced by the shank.

Fig. 76. Flexible shank

4. *The filler* – in welted, sewn or cemented construction, a layer of
    filler is placed in the shallow cavity underneath the insole
    bounded by the edges of the upper to provide a smooth surface
    for sole attaching (see Fig. 76). It also provides insulation for the
    foot from the ground and can 'bed down' to the shape of the
    foot with wear.

Size and width markings

Three size scales apply to footwear sold in the United Kingdom –
United Kingdom, American and Continental (Paris points).

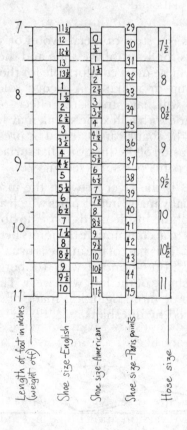

Fig. 77. Sizing systems of ladies shoes

United Kingdom

The UK scale starts at size 0 equivalent to a foot measurement of 102mm (4in) and has 8½mm (⅓in) between whole sizes (4mm 1/6in) between half sizes). Size 13 is reached at length 212mm (8⅓in). The scale restarts at size 1 (adults) at 220mm (8⅔in). The intervals between sizes are the same.

The distance round the last at the ball of the foot (girth) increases by 5mm (3/16in) for whole sizes up to children's size 10, and 6.5mm (¼in) for whole sizes above this. The girth of each size is not fixed, and the shoe can be designated a certain width fitting despite small variations in this measurement. Shoes can be made in 7 standard widths labelled A to G – A being the narrowest. Sometimes, in men's shoes, numbers 1 to 7 are used instead. Shoes that are made in only one width are usually D (4) size. The girth increase between fittings is normally 6.5mm (¼in) for adult footwear.

American

The American sizing system is slightly different. Ladies' shoes are marked 1½ sizes larger than their UK equivalent: for example, UK ladies 5½ equals American 7 or 70 (sizes are sometimes shown multiplied by 10). Men's shoes are marked ½ to 1 size larger, for example, UK men's 8 equals American 8½ or 9.

Width variations are similar but start at Triple A which is equivalent to A in the UK system.

Continental (Paris Points Scale)

This scale begins at 0 and increases by 6.5mm (¼in) per size. For example, UK ladies' 5½ equals Continental size 38/39. Most continental shoes do not show a width marking. When made in one width only, they are likely to be narrower than the average UK fitting.

These sizing systems provide a guideline only. Each manufacturer has his own version of each size and individual last shapes also differ. For this reason, people should, instead of stating which size of shoe they want, ask the assistant to measure their feet and use his or her knowledge of the manufacturer's variations to help give the correct fitting.

Measurement

Where possible, measurements for shoes should always be taken when standing as the foot expands in length and width as weight is taken on it. If this is not possible, the body weight can be simulated by pressing firmly with the measuring gauge as the foot is measured. Both feet should always be measured.

Many people do not realise that few adults remain the same shoe size throughout maturity. The arch structure may elongate slightly requiring a longer shoe, or the width of the foot may vary as weight is gained or lost and may even vary from morning to evening. For these reasons people should be strongly advised to have their feet measured every time they buy shoes.

Shopping for shoes

Some manufacturers try to provide a full range of sizes and fittings, others specialise in broad, narrow or large shoes. When looking for a particular style or fitting, people can be advised to write to manufacturers specialising in the fitting required asking for a catalogue and lists of local stockists. This can save endless wandering from shop to shop. Unfortunately, even this method does not always solve the problem, as to stock just one of each size is a large capital outlay; most shops therefore cater for those with average feet, although they will order sizes not stocked. Some manufacturers operate a mail order service and although it may be difficult to obtain a correct fit when buying shoes in this way, mail order does provide a service for elderly or immobile people who may find it difficult to visit a shop.

A list of manufacturers who make special fittings or sizes is available on receipt of a stamped addressed envelope from the Disabled Living Foundation (see Appendix III for the address).

Factors affecting fit

1. *Shoe flare*
    Left and right shoes were originally made identical to make the feet look symmetrical. It was then found that a pair of shoes

fitted more comfortably if the left and right were shaped differently. Because of this, most shoes are now 'in-flared' to some degree (see Fig. 78). The degree of 'in-flare' varies from shoe to shoe and different angles will suit different people.

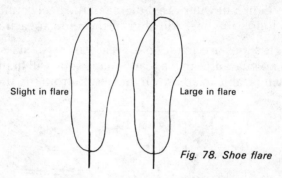

Slight in flare   Large in flare

Fig. 78. Shoe flare

2.   *Inside border*
The shape of the toe of the shoe affects its appearance but the longest point of the foot is usually the first or second toe and, if shaping starts before the end of the toes, these toes will be pushed inwards (see Fig. 79). This is particularly disadvantageou to someone with a tendency towards *hallux valgus*.

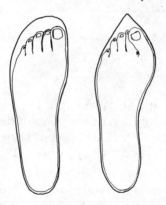

Fig. 79. Effect on toes of shaped inside border

3.   *Heel to ball of the foot measurement*
People who have longer toes than others need to find shoes with a correspondingly long forepart (see Fig. 80). A fitter, after gauging the length of the instep by measuring the distance from

the heel to the ball of the foot, will be able to advise on the most comfortable footwear.

4. *Heel shape*
    The heel of the foot should fit snugly into the heel of the shoe. Too tight a fit will cause bulging of the heel counter and, if it is too loose, the heel will shift in the shoe at each step.

Although shoes are made in a great variety of sizes and fittings, there is no guarantee that a ready-made shoe will fit properly. Shoe fitters will be able to advise on the best fit from the shoes available.

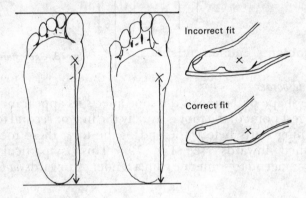

Fig. 80. Measurement from the heel to the ball of the foot

Fitting problems

Toe deformities and also present fitting problems as extra depth in the front of the shoe is required. Depth depends on the girth of the last (see page 93). Extra deep lasts are used by some manufacturers in certain styles (see page 173).

Some of the most awkward fitting problems are posed by people who have narrow heels and wide forefeet. No standard footwear is available to accommodate feet shaped in this way; the only answer is to buy laced or bar shoes which are wide enough to fit the forefeet. Such a shoe will be too big at the heel, but adequate fastening, with perhaps the addition of a pad under the tongue, will help to keep the foot back in the shoe.

The foot with the high instep is also difficult to fit. Often a shoe with a bar will be more comfortable than a lace.

'Wearing in'

Many older people maintain that shoes have to be 'worn in'. It is true that leather uppers will become moulded to the shape of the feet (see page 88) and shoes constructed with filler between the sole and the insole will become slightly bigger as the filler 'beds down' with wear. It is also true that shoes with stitched on soles ease slightly with use but most modern constructions, including all those with synthetic uppers and moulded soles, will not 'wear in' at all. This is another reason why people should be encouraged to have their feet measured and buy shoes which fit.

Foot problems caused by shoes

Contrary to common belief, the idea that the shoe is the main cause of irreversible foot deformities is not true. The fact that many people who wear 'unsuitable' footwear throughout life have perfectly shaped feet bears this out.

No two people have the same shaped feet. Due to these variations some feet will be more likely to develop foot problems than others and ill-fitting footwear undoubtedly hastens the onset of foot problems in these feet. For example, *hallux valgus* was often attributed to wearing unsuitable shoes in the past but this deformity is also found in people who have never worn shoes. It is often found in people with a particular bone shape (see page 12). Those born with this bone shape are therefore likely to develop *hallux valgus* whatever shoes they wear although wearing unsuitable footwear is likely to accelerate and increase the severity of this condition.

It is also true to say that many painful lesions would not be present if it were not for shoes. Corns and callosites (see page 25) are caused by wearing ill-fitting shoes, but as these lesions are a direct result of pressure and friction currently being exerted, they can easily be cured by changing to correctly fitting footwear.

Most people do not feel discomfort from badly fitting shoes in proportion to the pressure exerted. Thus the problem is not brought to people's attention until the callosity (which forms to protect the area) thickens, and causes pain. The footwear is not suspected as the cause.

If shoes are too big or not held in place by a lace or a bar (see page 99), the shoe will tend to fall off at each step and the toes will grip hard to keep it on. Habitual curling of the toes for this reason can lead to toe deformity.

Children's toes constricted by socks or shoes which are too small will become fixed in the curled up position, but these deformities will correct themselves as the child grows providing the cause is removed. Adults who consistently wear hose or shoes that are too small may also develop a deformity as the soft tissue structures become shortened.

Fashion

Throughout history, people have endured all kinds of physical discomfort for the sake of fashion and status. Perhaps the worst example of this was the Chinese custom of binding the feet of children so that they grew up with tiny feet. More recently, winkle-pickers and platform soles have caused similar discomfort.

Most fashion shoes do not fit the foot properly. Like all items of fashion, shoes are an illusion of how people would like their feet to look, thus the shoe shape does not conform to the shape of the feet. The lasts of women's shoes in particular are made narrower and deeper (see Fig. 81) than the foot they are designed for to give the shoe a lighter, more elegant line.

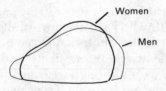

Fig. 81. A woman's last – narrower and deeper than the foot it is designed for

However new a fashion may seem, shoe designers work on only eight basic styles of shoe, all of which have been in existence for a long time. Most variations occur in toe shapes and in the shapes, heights and positions of heels.

Apart from the obvious harmful effects of bad shape and lack of adequate fastening, fashion shoes have the added problem that they seldom fit well. Many imported shoes are manufactured in only one width – medium. To be competitive, British manufacturers cut down on the number of lasts for each shoe and, even when a number are available, the retailer can afford to stock only a few variations. So great is the desire to follow fashion that poor fit does not deter people from wearing fashion shoes and this can damage some people's feet. If comfort and fashion cannot be combined in the same shoe, people should be encouraged to have a pair of each type and keep the less comfortable ones for special occasions.

Suitable shoes

The ideal shoe should be long enough and deep enough to avoid putting any pressure on the tips or tops of the toes and there should be about 1 cm (⅜in) between the longest toe and the inside front of the shoe.

The shoe should have a firm fastening around the instep (a lace or a bar) so that, when fastened, the heel of the foot fits snugly into the back of the shoe and is held there so that the foot is unable to slip forward into the shaped toe section (see Fig. 82). Lack of fastening allows the foot to slip forward and the heel will tend to slip out of the shoe as the foot is lifted (walking out). Anyone with this problem assumes that the shoes are too big and buys a smaller pair. Shoes of this kind, therefore, tend to be worn too short, so that the toes are forced to conform to the shaped toe section.

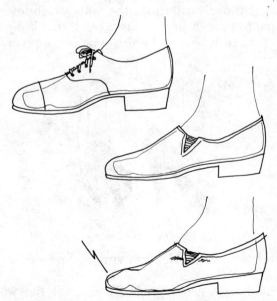

Fig. 82. The effect of a lace or a bar holding the foot back in the shoe

Not all slip-on shoes have this drawback. Slip-on shoes with open fronts will not compress the toes and slip-on shoes can also be most useful for people who find difficulty in bending down to tie laces or fasten buckles. The higher the shoe comes up around the instep, the better the support will be. For this reason, footwear which has been adapted to slip-on, for example elastic used to lace up a shoe or buckles attached with elastic (see page 161), will be better than a standard slip-on as they come well up the instep.

Another factor affecting the suitability of a shoe is its age. A pair of shoes worn continuously over a long period of time may become unsuitable due to deterioration of the compounds.

Heel height

Most people are accustomed to wearing a slight heel on their shoe and many find a completely flat heel uncomfortable. Even a modest heel will throw the weight of the foot forward in the shoe and, unless restrained, the foot will tend to slip down into the toe part of the shoe. Thus it is even more important when wearing a shoe with a modest to high heel to have a lace or a bar to keep the heel of the foot back in the shoe.

Excessively high heels will throw the body weight even further forward so that too much pressure is taken through the forefoot. The walking pattern is altered by this type of footwear, stride is

Fig. 83. Effect of worn heels

shortened heel cord (achilles tendon) and will find walking barefoot heel/toe action.

People who have worn high heels all their life will have a shortened heel cord *(achilles tendon)* and will find walking barefoot or in low heels uncomfortable; also their balance may be impaired. Such factors must be taken into consideration when advising on suitable shoes or assessing a person's walking ability or balance.

Another factor affecting balance is wearing down the outside edges of heels. This means that the shoe is no longer a stable platform on which to walk. Wear has to be quite marked for low heels to be affected in this way, but worn high heels accentuate the problem (see Fig. 83).

Slippers (see Fig. 84)

The reasons why slippers are said to be bad for people to wear is not that they give 'no support'. Many slippers have no method of fastening and therefore do not grip the foot adequately. They are liable to slip off as easily as they slip on, possibly leading to a trip or a fall. Since they are seldom available in half sizes or alternative width fittings, they often fit only approximately. Slippers which tend to slip off encourage shuffling (see page 51), the calf muscles are not used efficiently and the feet and ankles may swell making it impossible to put on outdoor shoes. Wearing slippers all the time can decrease the incentive to be active and, if this is combined with wearing a dressing gown all day, lead to a lowering of morale and depression.

In an attempt to prevent slippers slipping off, they are worn short like casual shoes (see page 99). Although slipper uppers are soft, the constant pressure on the toes that this contact causes can still cause problems.

Some slipper soles wear out very quickly and are difficult to repair with the result that people may walk about in slippers with damaged soles which may cause the wearer to trip or fall. Falls may also be precipitated by slippers with plastic soles. Some of these appear to have a non-slip surface when new but this can, with comparatively little wear, become highly polished and slippery.

Corrective devices cannot be used in slippers as the material of which the slippers are made is too soft to allow the insole to work correctly. If slippers are worn for long periods indoors, the amount of time in which a prescribed device is worn is limited, for example to trips to the shops when wearing outdoor shoes.

Providing these factors are taken into consideration, there is no harm in wearing well fitting slippers for some part of each day.

People with awkwardly shaped feet may even walk better in slippers as they may be more comfortable than their outdoor shoes.

Fig. 84. Trodden-down 'slippers'

The best sort of slippers

The best slippers are those which enclose the heel and the forefoot and come as high up the forefoot as possible, allowing the foot to be gripped and diminishing the possibility of the slipper falling off. The elasticated gusset type are suitable providing the elastic has not become lax and people are not tempted to slip on only the toe portion and not put the heel in. Better than these are the zip-up variety of slipper or the less common lacing variety (see Fig. 85).

Lightweight washable zip-to-toe slippers are available in standard or bootee style (see Fig. 86) from two orthopaedic footwear manufacturers (Camp Ltd and P R Cooper (Footline) Ltd (see Appendix II for addresses)). These come in standard depths but Camp Ltd will supply an extra deep fitting or odd sizes at no extra cost. A similar slipper with a shorter zip and warm lining is supplied by Damart (see Appendix II). The lace-up variety shown in Figure 85 is supplied by the Bury Boot and Shoe Co Ltd.

If this type of slipper cannot be used for any reason, for example if someone has difficulty in bending down to put slippers on, a type of German exercise sandal (Birkenstock Sandal) has proved to be a useful compromise. These slip-on sandals are available in several styles but all have a high instep strap and deep cork footbed which prevent the sandal from slipping off (see Appendix II for the address).

Slippers with a fleecy lining will keep feet warm, but they must be large enough so that the lining is not compressed squeezing out the insulating layer of air diminishing its warming effect.

Fig. 85. Lace-up slipper

A person who has to spend long periods in the house, should try not to wear slippers continuously, but either wear outdoor shoes for a few hours every day or buy a pair of lightweight indoor shoes (e.g. a well fitting sandal which supports the back of the heel and laces or buckles across the instep). These or a pair of soft fabric shoes (for example, corduroy) can be changed into indoors.

People should also be reminded to check the soles of their slippers regularly for wear or signs that the soles are getting slippery. This point could also be checked when patients are admitted to hospital.

Fig. 86. Zip-to-toe slippers

Other shoe problems

Allergy to shoe components

Allergy to any element used in shoe construction can make buying shoes very difficult. This is a rare condition. The symptoms of an allergic reaction may present with red, itchy skin or a severe burning sensation and the only cure is never to wear that particular shoe or any constructed in the same way again. The cause of the allergy is often clear from the distribution of the symptoms, for example an allergy to a rubber sole would affect only the sole of the foot (see page 23).

Substances which sometimes cause this type of problem are:

1. the soling material, e.g. rubber;
2. the cement used in the construction of the shoes;
3. the dye used to colour the leather;
4. the chromate used in tanning leather.

Soles are made from many different substances so an allergy to a particular type is a fairly simple problem to solve. Several types of shoes are made without using cement in the construction (see page 85) but it is always advisable to contact the manufacturer to check that cement is not used in a particular shoe. This is particularly true of ladies' shoes, most of which are made by cement construction.

Allergies to the chemicals used in tanning or to shoe dyes are more difficult to alleviate as most leathers, even those in natural colours, are treated in some way. One solution is to write to the Shoe and Allied Trades Research Association (see Appendix III for address) who may be able to advise about specific problems.

Different sized shoes

Many people experience difficulty getting shoes to fit because they have feet of slightly different sizes. Adaptations which make shoes of the same size suitable are discussed in the next chapter.

If the difference is greater than two sizes, shoes of different sizes should be bought as the structure of the shoe is designed to be flexible at a certain point (over the ball of the foot) and the shorter foot will be trying to bend where the shoe is more rigid. The problem can sometimes be overcome (see page 142).

Odd pairs of shoes can be bought from certain manufacturers. These odd pairs usually cost more than an ordinary pair and there is usually a delay while the shoes are manufactured because, to match exactly, a pair of shoes must be cut from the same skin and have the same sole thickness. Colours and styles are necessarily limited. A list of manufacturers prepared to offer this service can be obtained from the Disabled Living Foundation (see Appendix III).

Various associations have been set up, to try to pair individuals with corresponding odd feet. The benefit of such schemes is that the participants pay only for one pair of shoes. However, finding partners whose taste and colour preference and foot size and fitting are identical can be difficult. Addresses of these associations can be found in Appendix II. Manufacturers affiliated to one of these associations offer two pairs of shoes at discount prices to the association members. The unwanted odd pairs of shoes can then be advertised in the association's journal.

Many of the ready-made special shoes (see page 107) can be supplied in odd sizes, although difference in size of feet alone is not a valid reason for having these supplied by a hospital.

The problem of odd sized feet can also be solved by having shoes made to measure. Made-to-measure shoes can be very expensive but there are made-to-measure services using adapted standard lasts which are only slightly more expensive than ordinary good quality footwear (see page 117).

Swollen feet

Buying shoes for swollen feet or those which tend to swell can be difficult as the size may alter by several sizes at different times of the day. In general, the feet will be larger in the evening than in the morning so shoes should be purchased as late in the day as possible. The most important feature to look for in a shoe is adjustability. A lace-up shoe will be better than a bar as it will exert a more even pressure. Standard footwear does not offer any adjustment in the toe part and a low lacing style (see Fig. 87) may be more comfortable. Few shoes of this type are commercially available although there is one which is marketed through a mail order company (see Appendix II). Two ready-made orthopaedic shoes offer a choice of low lacing (see pages 110 and 112), and adaptations can be carried out either to extend the lacing of a standard shoe or make the shoe more comfortable (see page 138).

Fig. 87. Low lacing shoe and sandal

Provision of orthopaedic footwear

Orthopaedic footwear, adaptations to patients' own footwear when necessary and a repair service for both of these are provided through the National Health Service hospitals. Some hospitals have their own workshops but most orthopaedic footwear is made through commercial firms under contract to the Department of Health and Social Security.

The consultant in charge of the patient will prescribe orthopaedic footwear or footwear adaptations when necessary. Guidelines are laid down by the Department of Health and Social Security for the provision of footwear by the National Health Service (see *Provision of medical and surgical appliances handbook* Appendix IV). These state that footwear can only be supplied in cases of foot deformity when standard footwear is not suitable and cannot be adapted. Footwear cannot be supplied for cases of uneven leg length, odd sized feet or when special footwear is needed due to allergy unless built in surgical features are also needed.

The contractor's orthotist attends the hospital clinic and sends the measurements to the company's factory where shoes are either supplied from stock or made to measure.

Orthopaedic footwear is free, and when clinical need can be fulfilled by adapting the patient's own footwear, this is carried out free of charge. Repairs to orthopaedic footwear are also free.

Under present regulations, two pairs of surgical footwear can be supplied at one time if necessary, and a third pair may be authorised where there are strong medical or occupational grounds. Up to three pairs of shoes may be adapted initially, and a further pair after a year, or when the need arises. Such footwear should be ordered some months before it is needed to allow for delay.

Orthopaedic footwear

Orthopaedic footwear can be divided into two groups:

1. ready-made footwear made on extra deep and/or extra wide lasts;
2. made-to-measure footwear.

1. Ready-made orthopaedic footwear

There are several types of ready-made orthopaedic footwear and within each type there are a variety of different makes and styles of shoe. Some are wider, deeper, lighter or softer than others and the full range of footwear currently available has been included to demonstrate the wide choice.

(i) Extra wide and extra deep shoes – the removable insoles supplied enable the wearer to increase the width and depth if necessary

All these shoes are suitable for orthopaedic alterations and can be supplied in odd sizes, some at extra cost.

(a) *Radus Surgical Shoes* – supplied by Ken Hall Ltd
Sizes: wide range.
Widths: narrow, medium, wide and very wide.
Depths: deep – adjustable with 2 insoles.
Fastening: laces.
Upper: leather.
Sole: lightweight, synthetic material.

Insoles: two plastazote insoles which can be removed or moulded to fit.
Colour: mid brown and black; others available at extra charge.
Odd Sizes: available at extra cost.

(b) *Nustyle Shoe* (Ladies) – supplied by Ken Hall Ltd

Sizes: whole sizes only from 1 upwards.
Widths: normal and wide.
Depths: deep, adjustable with 2 insoles.
Fastening: lace.
Upper: suede or calf leather.
Sole: microcellular (other materials, e.g. leather, on request).
Insoles: 1, 6.5mm (¼in) Poron, 1, 6.5mm (¼in) medium density plastazote.
Colour: brown, mushroom, blue, beige (suede – 2-tone colour).
Odd sizes: available at extra cost.

Note: A Nustyle shoe is also available for men.

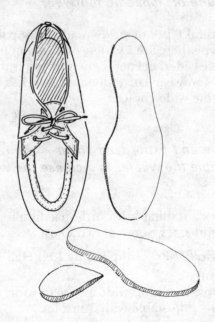

Fig. 88. Orthopaedic shoe with removable insoles

(c) *Multifit Shoe* – supplied by Kettering Surgical Applicances Ltd
(see Fig. 88)

Sizes: women's 2 to 8; men's 6 to 11.
Widths: wide and extra wide.
Depths: deep, but extra depth if one or more insoles are removed.
Fastening: normally lacing. The leather version can be supplied
with velcro.
Upper: suede or calf leather.
Sole: Microcellular.
Insole: built-in triple insoles which can be removed in full or half
sections. The insoles allow 13mm (½in) extra depth in the forepart
and 6.5mm (¼in) extra at heel.
Colour: beige, brown, black in suede; black or brown in calf.
Odd sizes: available.

Note: has an additional loose padding for the tongue.

(d) *Comfort Shoe* – supplied by LSB Orthopaedics Ltd

Sizes: 2 to 11 black or tan with option of 44-52mm (1¾in-2in) depth
at toe. 2 to 8 – suede.
Widths: good in the forepart of the shoe.
Depths: deep – adjustable by removing the insole.
Fastening: velcro strap.
Upper: leather and suede.
Lining: foam in the forepart.
Sole: microlite.
Insole: 8mm (5/16in) orthaton.
Colour: black or tan leather, mushroom suede with matching
leather trim.
Odd sizes: available at 25% extra cost.

Note: a soft version of the comfort shoe made of waterproof
material is also available. The front flap fastens with velcro.

(ii) Other shoes made on extra wide or extra deep lasts in a fixed
range of sizes

These can be worn with separate ready-made insoles or made-to-
measure insoles. All are also suitable for adaptation and most can
be supplied in odd sizes. Some are available with a longer opening
(Gibson lace to the toe) which is suitable for feet prone to swelling.

(a) *Camp Adult Shoe* – supplied by Camp Ltd (see Fig. 89)

Sizes: all.
Widths: normal, wide and extra wide.
Depths: deep and extra deep.
Fastening: lace – 3 eyelets.
Upper: leather.
Lining: foam in the forepart.
Sole: microcellular.
Insole: none.
Colour: black and brown.
Odd sizes: available at no extra charge.

(b) *Mo Shoe* – supplied by P. R. Cooper (Footline) Ltd
One of a range of lightweight special shoes

Sizes: all.
Widths: normal, medium and wide.
Depths: deep and extra deep.
Fastening: can be 3 eyelet or long opening lacing.
Upper: leather or man-made, breathable uppers.
Lining: foam in the forepart.
Sole: leather or micro-wedge soles. Heels can be fitted at slight extra cost.
Insole: not standard but can be supplied.
Colour: various.
Odd sizes: split sizes of length, width and depth available at no extra cost.

Note: also available in boot or sandal form (see Fig. 89).

(c) *Piedro Ladies Shoes* – supplied by Gilbert & Mellish Ltd

Sizes: 3 to 8 including half sizes.
Widths: one only.
Depths: one only.
Fastening: velcro or lace.
Upper: suede with leather trim.
Lining: leather in heel and quarters.
Sole: microcellular rubber.
Insole: none.
Colour: beige, blue or grey.
Odd sizes: available.

Note: A Piedro man's shoe is also available in sizes 6 to 11 including half sizes, velcro fastening only and a choice of black or brown colour.

Fig. 89. Examples of orthopaedic shoes with extra width

(iii) Shoes made in standard depths but several width fittings

Solidus Shoe – supplied by Orthopaedic Footwear Ltd
(James Taylor & Son)

One of a range of fashion shoes made in Germany and imported by some orthopaedic firms.

Sizes: 3 to 12.
Widths: from wide to very wide.
Depths: standard.
Fastening: lace.
Upper: leather.
Sole: leather.
Insole: padded leather.
Colour: black or fawn.
Odd sizes: not available.

Note: not all widths are available from all suppliers. One only, available from Orthopaedic Footwear Ltd. Other suppliers include Kettering Surgical Appliances.

(iv) Shoes made in standard depth and only one width fitting

(a) *Beta Shoe* – supplied by Dudley Surgical Appliances
One of a range of lightweight special footwear.

Sizes: 3 to 8.
Widths: one only.
Depths: standard.
Fastenings: lacing with low front opening.
Upper: leather.
Lining: foam in the forepart.
Sole: microcellular.
Insole: none.
Colour: black or brown.
Odd sizes: not available.

Note: A similar shoe, the *Alpha* shoe, is also available as above but with a standard front opening. Boots are available in both styles.

(b) *Soft Shoes* – supplied by Remploy

Sizes: 2 to 8.
Width: one only.
Depth: one only.
Fastening: lace or velcro.
Upper: water resistant stiffened canvas.
Sole: microcellular.
Colour: brown or black.
Odd sizes: available at 20% surcharge.

(v) Plastazote shoes

These washable, lightweight special shoes are suitable for awkwardly shaped feet as they can be moulded to fit. Small areas can be shaped by spot heating (for example, with a hair dryer) and for more extensive changes the entire shoe can be placed in a special (plastazote) oven and then moulded to the foot when warm. As the material cools it sets into the moulded position giving a comfortable fit.

These shoes can be worn out of doors but are not suitable for orthopaedic adaptations.

Drushoe – supplied by John Drew (see Fig. 90)

Sizes: standard 1 to 11.
Widths: one only – very wide.
Depths: deep but extra depth available in sizes 4 to 11.
Fastening: wrap-over velcro.

Upper: seamless, thermoplastic material.

Sole: polyurethane.

Insole: comes with 2 plain insoles which can be moulded separately.

Colour: black, brown and fawn.

Odd sizes: supplied but size can be altered by varying the insole.

Note: the uppers can be cut away to form a sandal or to take pressure off a sore area. Punching holes in the front can make them attractive and also help to keep the foot cool.

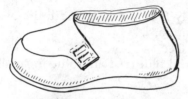

Fig. 90. Plastazote shoe

Fig. 91. An open-to-toe boot

(vi) Ready-made boots

Some people need the extra support at the ankle provided by boots and a number of ready-made boots are available. The choice is large up to adult size 5, but many boots are not available in larger sizes although some companies will supply these on request.

Some have openings which are extended to the toe by means of a strap across the bottom of the tongue (see Fig. 91). This is useful when sensation is impaired and it is necessary to feel the toes inside the boot to check that they are lying flat. All are suitable for orthopaedic adaptations and some are available in odd sizes.

(a) *The Piedro Boot* – supplied by Gilbert & Mellish

Sizes: from 19 to 45 in continental sizes (approximately size 3 to adult 10).
Widths: approximately D E and F (D width not available in red).
Depth: one only – standard.
Fastening: hook and lace.
Colour: brown, red and blue (red and blue in smaller sizes only).
Odd sizes: supplied.

(b) *Surgical Boot* – supplied by Orthopaedic Footwear Ltd
(James Taylor & Son)

Sizes: adult 4 to 12 in half sizes.
Width: approximately C.
Depth: one only – standard.
Fastening: eyelet and lace.
Colour: black.
Odd sizes: available.

(c) *The Biffabout Boot* – supplied by Ken Hall Ltd

Sizes: infant 1 to adult 9.
Width: very wide.
Depths: standard very deep, a slightly less deep fitting is also available.
Fastening: hook and lace.
Colour: brown– standard. Red, blue or mushroom can be supplied in smaller sizes.
Upper: suede or leather with warm plaid lining.
Odd sizes: supplied in brown suede or leather only.

(d) *The Hill Boot* – made to order by Remploy

Sizes: infant 0 to adult 11.
Widths: to order.
Depths: to order.
Fastening: hook and lace.
Colour: brown.

Upper: suede with warm plaid lining.
Odd sizes: supplied at 20% surcharge.

Other boots available in small sizes (up to adult 5/6) can be
obtained from Camp Ltd., P. R. Cooper (Footline) Ltd (will supply
larger sizes on request), Kettering Surgical Appliances Ltd, LSB
Orthopaedics Ltd., Myron Medical, The Orthotic Workshop at
Chailey Heritage and R. Taylor and Sons.

(vii) *Soft boots* (see Fig. 92)

Soft boots, traditionally made of felt although washable materials
are now being used by some manufacturers, are useful for
mobilising patients with bulky dressings following surgery or
those who have a swollen painful joint. Made on deep lasts, they can
be worn with insoles. Some are suitable for indoor wear only, but
others can be worn outside and are suitable for orthopaedic
adaptations. All have wide openings, some lace almost to the toe
and some are available with velcro fastenings.

Washable boots are supplied by Cumbria Orthopaedic Ltd. and
P. R. Cooper (Footline) Ltd. (These boots are only suitable for
indoor wear.) Other boots are supplied by Camp Ltd., Ellis Son and
Paramore, Kettering Surgical Appliances Ltd., LSB Orthopaedics
Ltd., Ken Hall and Remploy Ltd.

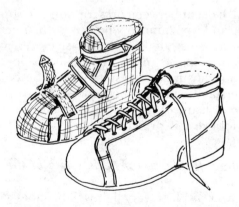

Fig. 92. Soft boots

2. Made-to-measure footwear (Bespoke)

(i) Shoes made to measure using traditional methods and materials

This type of orthopaedic footwear, necessary when none of the ready-made orthopaedic shoes are suitable, is made individually and all the orthopaedic features needed by the patient are incorporated into it from the beginning. Besides fitting over deformities and correcting functional disorders, this type of footwear can be designed with patients' particular problems in mind, for example skin sensitivity or vascular disturbances.

The style and method of construction will vary according to the needs of each patient. The sturdy welted shoe (see page 85) was preferred in the past for its durability but the newer cement constructions have allowed much lighter shoes to be made which are just as durable. Any of the footwear adaptations described in Chapter 9 can be incorporated into these shoes. Supports to compensate for a shorter leg or to redistribute body weight are pre-shaped over the last before the sole is applied. Extra stiffening can also be incorporated into the part of the shoe containing the heel of the foot (the counter) or the outside edges of the base of the upper. Only the best quality materials are used. Leather is used almost exclusively for the uppers and many soles, although the lighter weight synthetic soling materials are being used more and more.

The delays which occur between prescription and supply and the unsatisfactory fit and appearance which is sometimes the result have led to criticisms of this expensive service, costing approximately four times as much as a ready-made orthopaedic shoe. There are no statistics on the suitability of bespoke footwear but a better understanding of the methods of construction and the built-in orthopaedic features can only help to ensure that the most suitable type of footwear is prescribed.

(ii) Shoes moulded on plaster-of-Paris casts of the foot

For particularly awkward feet, very lightweight shoes can be made by moulding the upper directly onto a plaster cast of the foot (see Fig. 93). This is not as easy a way of making shoes as it sounds because, unless modifications are made to the cast before moulding, the shoe will tend to be too short and will be too loose at the heel. Allowances must be made for the change in shape of the foot during walking (see page 83).

P. R. Cooper (Footline) Ltd offers shoes (Footline Shoes) which are made in this way in a range of styles, colours and upper materials.

Fig. 93. Shoe made on a plaster-of-Paris cast

(iii) Shoes made to measure on adapted standard lasts (semi-bespoke shoes)

A cheaper and simpler method of making a pair of shoes to fit an individual's measurements involves adapting standard lasts and this avoids the need to design a specific last for each foot. These shoes can be made to fit over many awkward deformities which make buying standard footwear impossible but for which orthopaedic adaptation is not necessary, for example *hallux valgus*. They can also be made in odd sizes or with the extra depth necessary to incorporate an insole.

Several companies now offer this type of service but perhaps the best known is the 'John Locke' shoe (see Fig. 94). These shoes are now made by two companies (see Appendix II), one of which markets through some retail shops and the other through some orthotists for the National Health Service. Measurements are taken by a qualified fitter and sent to the factories to be made up. Other firms offer a similar service via mail order – the customer taking his own measurements. Accurate measurements are essential for good fit and it is more satisfactory, when possible, for the customer to visit the shoemaker for direct measurement.

Fig. 94. 'John Locke' shoe

Rehabilitation footwear

This type of footwear is not prescribed but is usually loaned to patients who are recovering from operations.

There are two types:

those with a rigid sole used to immobilise the foot immediately after the operation;

those with a semi rigid sole to allow a little movement of the foot used in the latter stages of rehabilitation.

Both types have velcro strap or lace fastenings to allow maximum adjustment over a heavily bandaged foot (see Fig. 55, page 61).

A third type of boot is worn over a plaster-of-Paris cast on the foot to allow weight bearing on the plaster after it is set.

This type of footwear can be obtained from Dudley Surgical Appliances, Orthopaedic Systems, Pryor and Howard and other firms. See Appendix II for addresses.

Temporary footwear

There are many reasons why elderly people experience difficulty in walking. Sometimes there will be no apparent cause, sometimes specific or multiple pathology can be pinpointed. One reason for immobility which can be avoided is lack of suitable footwear; an elderly person may be waiting for orthopaedic footwear to be delivered or be undergoing treatment for an ulcer on the foot when bandages make the fitting of ordinary footwear impossible. In situations like these, some alternative footwear must be provided as a temporary loss of mobility in elderly people can soon become permanent.

When the foot is heavily bandaged and weight-bearing is allowed, it is most important that a non-slip surface for the sole is provided. The easiest way of providing this is to turn a piece of foam-padded stockinette (tubipad) inside out and pull it on over the bandage with the foam surface forming a sole. Care must be taken to ensure that the tubipad is large enough to avoid constricting the bandage. Several sizes are available from Seton (see Appendix II).

An alternative to tubipad is a foam slipper that stretches. These, also available in a number of sizes (supplied by Henley's Medical Supplies, see Appendix II), can be pulled on over a bandaged foot.

Both the tubipad and the foam slipper provide temporary, flat, non-slip surfaces; both can be washed although care must be taken to see that the tubipad has not shrunk. With constant use both will show signs of wear and, when this happens, a more permanent solution should be considered.

Another method of providing a non-slip surface for short walks is a detachable sole which can be fixed with velcro to a type of wrap-around sheepskin bootee slipper (see Fig. 95). Many patients being nursed in bed wear this sort of boot to prevent pressure sores; they can attach the sole when getting out of bed. Such slippers are available from Dermalex (see Appendix II).

Fig. 95. Lambpad slipper showing removable sole

When the condition which prevents ordinary shoes being worn is likely to continue for some time – for example, when the forefoot is tender following amputation of the toes – or during the period of waiting for bespoke orthopaedic footwear, a more permanent solution must be considered.

One such solution involves making a temporary sandal out of a heat-moulded material (plastazote); this is usually done in physiotherapy or occupational therapy departments. Shaped layers of plastazote (see pattern, Fig. 96) are heated in a special oven and then moulded round the patient's foot. This provides quite serviceable indoor sandals, after heel pieces have been stuck on and velcro stitched to the fronts. This type of footwear is very light and is particularly suitable for sensitive feet. When the toes are vulnerable, a toecap can be moulded separately and stuck on to protect them.

A simpler remedy is to open the front and back seams of a bootee-style slipper and sew on velcro straps with adjustable ring fastenings (see Fig. 97) which can be adjusted to give a good fit over any thickness of bandage.

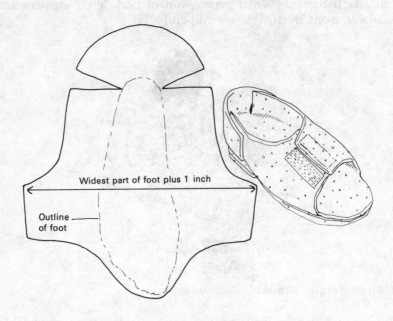

Widest part of foot plus 1 inch

Outline of foot

Fig. 96. Hand-made plastazote shoe and pattern

If an outdoor shoe is required, the flexible soled form of rehabilitation footwear (see page 118) may be suitable, although it will not protect the foot from damp conditions. A do-it-yourself shoe, like the one devised by the Association of Chartered Physiotherapists in *Geriatric Medicine,* which can be made to fit over any shape of foot (see Fig. 98) may be the answer. A pattern from which such a shoe can be made is available from the Clothing Adviser at the Disabled Living Foundation (see Appendix III for the address) on receipt of a stamped addressed envelope.

The possibilities for temporary footwear are varied – only some have been described to indicate what can be done given adequate resources. The importance of some form of footwear to prevent people becoming immobile just because they are unable to wear shoes cannot be overstressed.

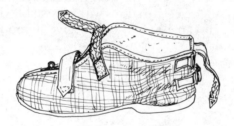

Fig. 97. Adapted slipper

Fig. 98. 'Do-It-Yourself' shoe

Commercially available footwear

It is not possible to list the many types of commercially available footwear which may be suitable for some problem feet. Certain types of footwear are often available commercially, for example laced sandals with filled-in heels made by a number of manufacturers in the summer months.

Some normal footwear which has been found to be particularly suitable is marketed by the Bury Boot and Shoe Company (see Appendix II for the address). This company offers a range of broader, deeper shoes which are available by mail order. They also make a low lacing shoe 'the Extra Special Shoe' and a lacing sandal like the one described above.

9

Orthoses (Appliances) and Footwear Adaptations

Orthotics is the relatively new term given to the fitting and making of calipers, splints and other orthopaedic appliances (orthoses). It aims to simplify descriptions of commonly used items by referring to the joints on which they act. For example, a full length caliper can be described as a knee-ankle foot orthosis (KAFO) and a below knee caliper as an ankle-foot orthosis (AFO). This section describes the most common forms of AFO and foot orthoses and how they affect footwear and walking ability.

Before describing the different types which are available, it is important to set out the limitations of such devices. While they can help to maintain a correction brought about by surgery or help to prevent deformity from progressing any further, they cannot normally be used to **correct** deformity as the forces necessary to correct the position of the part will damage the overlying tissue.

Ankle foot orthoses (AFOs)

The most common form of AFO prescribed is the foot-drop splint which helps to control foot drop, for example following stroke (hemiplegia). Which one is chosen of the many different types will depend largely on the condition of the foot to be splinted.

For those who are making a rapid recovery, a temporary splint will enable a normal walking pattern to be adopted straight away. These splints, which are usually flexible and either clip on to a standard shoe (see Fig. 99) or fit inside it, are not very strong but prevent the foot from dragging on the ground during walking and teach the patient what it feels like to put the heel down first at each step. Such splints can be used temporarily in both types of muscle condition found following stroke (spasticity and flaccidity) and are discarded as soon as the normal walking pattern is achieved unaided.

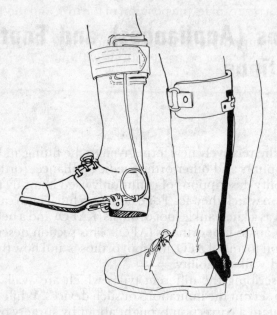

Fig. 99. Temporary foot drop orthoses — shoe clasp and clip varieties

Other types have rigid uprights and may be fitted with a joint allowing movement to occur over the region of the ankle joint. The shoe is adapted by inserting sockets (see page 133) into the heel into which the splint fits.

A further type is a moulded plastic splint made to conform to the patient's lower limb. This splint, which fits inside the shoe (probably larger in size than usual), can be used for an ankle that is floppy or stiff (flaccid or spastic) but is more useful for controlling the floppy ankle. It is not strong enough to control an ankle which tends to twist in or push down strongly (inversion or strong plantarflexion).

AFOs are also used to control ankle instability. A single iron combined with a T-strap which applies three-point pressure to keep the ankle in a good position (see Fig. 100) is usually sufficient. For example, for a *valgus* ankle an iron would be positioned down the outside of the lower leg and fitted into a socket in the shoe (see page 133). The T-strap is fitted to the inside of the shoe and buckles round the outside of the iron, holding the ankle up in the neutral position. For a *varus* ankle, the position of the iron and the T-strap is reversed.

If a stronger support is needed, a second iron is added forming a double iron which may be used with or without a T-strap.

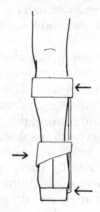

Fig. 100. T-strap and iron giving 3 point pressure

Insoles

Insoles (known in the shoe trade as inlays) are removable devices made to fit inside shoes and designed to redistribute body weight to relieve areas of pressure and friction. As with all orthoses, they must be worn with footwear that is sufficiently deep and wide to allow room for the insole and the patient's foot and cannot be worn with sandals or sling-backs in which the insole may move about and become wrongly aligned.

There are two types of insole – those which are made-to-measure and those which are supplied ready-made.

Made-to-measure insoles

Made-to-measure insoles are of three types: those moulded on the foot; those moulded on a plaster-of-Paris cast of the foot and those made in the form of previously applied padding.

Moulded on the foot   Insoles are often made of plastazote, a type of polythene foam which, when heated, becomes soft and malleable. Anyone standing on the material in this state can make a permanent imprint of the foot. Placing the insole inside the shoe cushions the pressure points.

One of the disadvantages of plastazote is that it is not a very durable material and, if worn repeatedly, loses its cushioning effect. Medium density plastazote has been found to last longer than the standard form. Another way of lengthening the life of plastazote insoles is by giving the patient two pairs and instructing him or her to wear them on alternate days and sponge them clean between wearings.

The thickness of the material can also cause problems as the insoles may be difficult to fit into standard footwear and a deeper pair of shoes may be necessary. The standard thickness of plastazote is 6mm (¼in). Greater cushioning can be achieved if thicker plastazote is used and some of the ready-made special shoes allow extra space for this type of insole (see page 107).

Moulded on a plaster-of-Paris cast   This type can be rigid or soft depending on the function for which the insole is intended. The cast is taken with the foot in a neutral position (one in which the subtalar joint is neither pronated or supinated) as in this position the foot is said to achieve optimal function. Corrective insoles are made in a firm material and are designed to keep the foot in the corrected position. Wedging ('posting') the insole involves building up and shaping the under-surface of the insole so that it allows the foot to move in a normal pattern during walking (see Fig. 101).

Soft insoles made of laminations of plastazote and rubbery materials like sorbothane or more permanent materials such as leather or cork could be made to redistribute the weight in a similar way to plastazote.

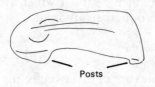

Posts

Fig. 101. Posted insole

Made in the form of previously applied padding Another type of soft made-to-measure insole is usually made by chiropodists (who also make many of the previous types). These insoles duplicate the action of padding and strapping which has previously been shown to relieve symptoms. The advantages of an insole over padding is that the patient does not have to return for frequent application of the padding and also the skin problems associated with the long-term use of adhesive strapping are avoided (see page 70).

Ready-made insoles

These insoles, available in a multitude of shapes, forms and materials, can be divided into two groups.

First, there are those made by orthopaedic appliance manufacturers to their most commonly requested patterns, for example, the Rose Taylor insole (see Fig. 102) (convex wedge insole, see page 10). A variety of sizes can be measured for and fitted immediately by the orthotist. The range of styles and materials in which these are made vary considerably from company to company. Most supply a range of cork and leather insoles with various degrees of padding under the arch and/or metatarsal heads.

Secondly, there is the range of insoles sold commercially in chemists and sports shops.

Fig. 102. Rose Taylor insole

Inserts

Inserts have a similar function to insoles, i.e. they redistribute the body weight in some way but do not extend to the full length of the foot. Common types of shoe inserts are metatarsal supports and heel pads.

The area underneath the metatarsal heads which becomes painful in a number of conditions (see Chapter 4) can be cushioned by pads. If the pain can be relieved by minimal padding a self-adhesive insert positioned inside an otherwise well fitting shoe can bring great relief. An alternative to this is to wear a pad attached to the foot by an elastic strap.

Care must be taken both in designing and fitting this type of insert as walking with a pad that is too hard or in the wrong place can cause damage.

Heel pads raise the heel slightly in the shoe which can relieve pain in conditions such as *achilles tendonitis* (page 2) or prevent chafing on the side of the foot. Heel pads can also be supplied in substances with special properties, for example sorbothane. This material is a shock absorber which can help to reduce the jarring encountered when walking on hard surfaces.

Problems associated with orthoses

Since many insoles and some orthoses are made of plastic material, they tend to make the feet sweat. This can be prevented if the patient:

1. washes his or her feet regularly and wears clean hose;
2. uses unperfumed anti-perspirant sprays;
3. uses a *little* talcum powder on the feet and in the splint;
4. wears socks made of materials which keep moisture away from the skin (wick) (see page 150);
5. wears *thin* cotton socks or stockinette inside plastic splints;

6. asks the orthotist to make ventilation holes in plastic orthoses. Patients should not make these holes themselves as they may weaken the splint.

Any orthoses worn close to the skin will need regular checking to make sure that it fits accurately. If, for any reason, it becomes too tight, excess pressure will be exerted on the skin and may lead to a sore. Patients should be warned to watch out for marks on the skin still present half an hour after removal of the splint (unlike the mark left by a watch strap, for example, which usually fades fairly rapidly).

Prosthetics

Prosthetics is the science of making and fitting appliances to replace a missing part of the body (prostheses).

In general, when a prosthesis is made to replace part of the leg, it is made individually to fit the patient and his or her footwear. This footwear is bought to fit the remaining foot and the prosthesis made to fit into this. Patients who have had one leg or part of it removed need to take particular care of the remaining foot and will need advice on footwear and footcare (see page 143).

Amputations of part of the foot are less common. They differ from amputations above the ankle in two ways – first, the prosthesis is not required to take the body's weight – just to provide balance and support for footwear; secondly, amputations through the ankle or back of the foot often leave a bulky stump which makes the wearing of standard footwear over the prosthesis difficult. Amputations through the mid-foot are particularly difficult because the operation cuts through some of the many muscles acting across this region leaving muscle imbalance, and the muscles which twist the foot downwards and inwards (plantarflexion and inversion) are left unopposed. This explains why these operations are rare and most amputations are done at a higher level where the blood and/or nerve supply is healthy and the difficulties of fitting the prosthesis fewer.

Amputation through the metatarsals is also rare, but this operation preserves all the main muscle groups leaving the ankle in balance and leaving a good weight-bearing surface so that a prosthesis is not really necessary. A toe filler in the gap in the shoe may be all that is required. The stump will again be slightly bulky and the shoe may have to be extra wide and deep. It is also important that a shoe is chosen which fastens as high up the instep as possible so that the stump is gripped firmly (see Fig. 103).

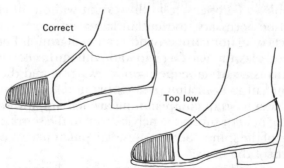

Correct

Too low

Fig. 103. A high vamped shoe to accommodate amputation of the metatarsals and toe filler

Standard footwear can usually be found to fit but the sole should be reinforced to make it more rigid to compensate for the missing part of the foot and prevent the toe filler pressing on the foot as the shoe bends.

In the early stages of rehabilitation of foot amputations, plastazote shoes (see page 112) will be most comfortable and will accommodate the post-operative swelling and bandaging.

Adaptations to footwear

Adaptations to standard footwear can solve a number of problems, for example by keeping the foot in a neutral position. Making fastening more manageable by adapting the lacing or using buckles or velcro and making the shoe open widely so that it can be put on more easily are other useful adaptations.

Adaptations to the soles and heels

Shoe raises

These are added to the soles and heels of shoes to even out differences in the length of the legs. This problem may have been present since childhood or may be a recent one due to an operation on the leg, for example a total hip replacement. Differences in length of less than one centimetre (⅜in) need no adaptation as the body is able to compensate to this extent without ill effect. Shoe raises will be necessary to even out larger differences as the long term effects of major compensation can be harmful. For example, one method of compensating is to walk with the heel of the short leg raised. This is an unstable position for walking and the ankle can become stiff in this position (shortening of the heel cord – *achilles tendon*). Other ways of compensating are walking with the knee of the long leg bent or tilting the pelvis down to the short side leading to twisting of the spine – both of these can put unnecessary strain on other parts of the body.

Blocks of wood of varying thicknesses can be used to find how high the raise needs to be to restore symmetry. The height needed is seldom as great as the difference in leg length.

Raises made of cork may be stuck on temporarily to see if they improve the walking pattern before the raise is made permanently in other materials. Raises up to 1 inch in height can be made out of a soling material such as microcellular rubber so that the shoe does not become too heavy. Raises thicker than this are usually made in cork or lightweight, high density materials such as plastazote or rigid polyeurathane foam which is covered in leather that matches the shoe. Another way of decreasing the weight of a raise is to make it with a waist so that there is a separate sole and heel portion to the raise. All shoe raises will increase the rigidity of the sole and make normal heel/toe walking difficult. To compensate for this, the toe section of the raise is usually slightly cut-away to allow the foot to rock forward on to this section as a step is taken. This action is similar to that of a rocker-sole (see page 132).

Wedged soles (see Fig. 104)

A wedge of soling material stuck to the edge of the sole of the shoe and tapering towards the middle can be used to correct sideways tilt at the ankle. It can be used on the inside to counteract inward rolling at the ankle *(valgus).* It is less effective if the forefoot is also rolled-in as the wedge tends only to lift this deformity. This adaptation may be combined with an extended heel (Thomas heel) or an insert designed to support the arch in the neutral position (*valgus* pad).

Wedged soles can also be used on the outside edge of the sole to counteract outward rolling of the ankle *(varus)* but this problem is less common.

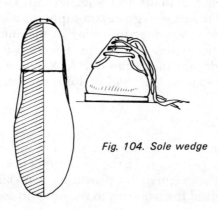

Fig. 104. Sole wedge

Floated heels (see Fig. 105)

A floated heel is one that extends the heel of the shoe outwards at its base increasing the area of the heel in contact with the ground. The effect of this is to discourage the heel from twisting as weight is taken. If a float is applied only to the inside surface it may help to discourage in-rolling of the ankle *(valgus)*. The back of the shoe must fit well and grip the heel of the foot for this adaptation, but, despite this, the foot tends to remain deformed within the shoe. A float out on both sides can help poor balance.

The function of the floated heels found on many training shoes is to prevent runners from twisting their ankles.

Fig. 105. Heel float

Elongated heel (Thomas heel)

In this adaptation, part of the heel is floated and extended along the inside border of the shoe to give extra support under the instep. It has been used to discourage in-rolling of the ankle *(valgus)* but, unless the shoe fits extremely well, the deformity is likely to occur within the shoe despite the extra support. A shoe with a wedge sole (one without a separate heel) will perform the same function.

A rocker sole

A rocker sole is used to prevent movement in stiff painful joints in the foot and ankle (for example, the big toe joint in *hallux rigidus*) and replace the lost movement by providing a rocking surface. As weight is transferred from one leg to the other in walking, the shoe rocks forward onto the cut-away front increasing the length of the stride. The heel of the shoe may need to be raised to maintain symmetry and also needs to be chamfered off at the edge (see Fig. 106).

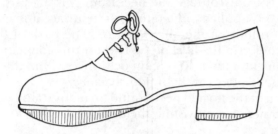

Fig. 106. Rocker sole

A lighter version of this adaptation uses a rocker bar. Since this provides the rocking action but does not protect the painful joint from moving, a rigid insole or extended steel sole plate may also be fitted to stiffen the sole. A similar adaptation consisting of a strip of cork or leather placed behind the ball of the foot (a metatarsal bar) is sometimes used to take some weight off this area if the forefoot is painful. These may, however, cause tripping and, for this reason, are seldom used.

Sockets and stops

When certain types of AFO are prescribed (see page 124) the heel of the shoe has to be adapted to accommodate the end of the appliance. This is done by inserting a metal tube in the heel of the shoe into which fits the ends of the appliance.

Sockets can be round or rectangular; round sockets allow full movement at the ankle in both directions – up (dorsiflexion) and down (plantarflexion) (see Fig. 107). Metal stops can be fitted in front or behind the socket to prevent movement in one direction. The back stop prevents downward movement at the ankle (plantarflexion) and may be fitted if the muscles which pull the foot up (dorsiflexors) are weak. The front stop prevents the upwards movement at the ankle (dorsiflexion). It is less frequently used but helps someone with weakness in the muscles which push down at the ankle (plantarflexion).

Rectangular or box sockets prevent movement in any direction. They are used in circumstances in which a back stop is used or when the appliance is fitted with an ankle joint.

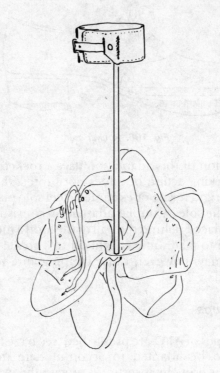

Fig. 107. Round socket allowing full movement

Valgus inserts

Prescribed to support an in-rolled ankle (*valgus* or pronated foot) in a more comfortable position, these inserts usually consist of a leather-covered, convex-shaped piece of cork which is attached inside the shoe in the position of the long arch. To be effective they must be fitted into a sturdy lace-up shoe which will help to maintain the corrected position.

Adaptations to shoe uppers

Stiffening

Extra pieces of stiffening material can be sewn into any area of the shoe to reinforce it if a deformity or a particular way of walking is causing excessive wear in that area. The most common site for extra stiffening is along the inside edge between the heel and the instep. This is often ordered at the same time as a *valgus* insert and helps to reinforce the corrected position.

Other upper modifications for comfort

The footwear adaptations described in this section are not confined to those done under prescription and, although an orthotist or chiropodist may arrange these modifications, they can also be done by experienced shoe repairers. All are designed to make an otherwise comfortable shoe fit over a deformity, for example a hammer toe, and can normally only be carried out successfully on shoes with leather uppers.

Shoe stretching   This modification may not even require the services of a shoe repairer as simple shoe stretching devices can be purchased for home use. The most common varieties used are the swan-neck shoe stretcher (see Fig. 108) or expandable lasts (see Fig. 109). Whatever the method, the aim is to provide a space in the upper large enough to fit over the deformity with comfort. The shoe must be worn for a few hours before stretching in order to isolate exactly the area to be enlarged. Softening solutions, which can be purchased commercially, can help if they are applied to the leather before the stretching operation is commenced.

Slit release   A slit release, which involves making several lengthways cuts in the upper close to the sole, has the effect of allowing the leather to stretch and gives extra width which can be useful in the forefoot when people have bunions. However, although such shoes are then no longer waterproof and should really only be worn indoors, they will be a safer form of foot covering than a slip-on slipper (see page 101) when comfortable shoes are hard to find.

Fig. 108. Swan-neck shoe stretcher

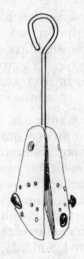

Fig. 109. Expandable last shoe stretcher

Balloon patching (see Fig. 110)   This modification involves cutting a large enough hole in the upper to allow the deformity, for example a bunion, to protrude through the hole. A leather patch is then placed over the hole and ballooned-out so that the bunion is enclosed but not constricted. This effective waterproof method of enlarging a shoe to accommodate a toe deformity can be almost unnoticeable once finished if matching leather is used.

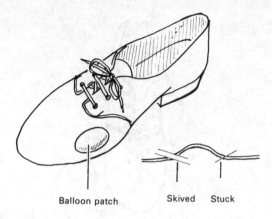

Balloon patch   Skived   Stuck

Fig. 110. Balloon patch

Lacing adaptations

Adaptations to the methods of fixing a shoe fall into two categories – those which extend the opening to make access to the shoe easier and those which make the fastening easier.

To improve the access to a shoe

For a number of reasons it may be convenient to have a shoe which unlaces right down to the toes. For example, when the toes are insensitive or paralysed, pushing the foot into a shoe may damage the toes or leave them curled up. It is important therefore to check that the toes are straight whenever the shoe is worn. Several ready-made special boots and shoes are made so that the opening comes right down to the toes (see page 113), but lacing can be similarly extended in ordinary footwear. On shoes which have an Oxford-style opening (see page 88), it is quite simple to make this adaptation; by unstitching the tongue from the base of the opening, the opening can be extended as far as required; extra eyelets are added down each side and the tongue is extended and re-attached preferably down one side of the opening. The adaptation is slightly more complicated on the Gibson-style shoe but can still be successful. In this case, the tongue is cut off level with the base of the old opening, a slit is then made down the centre of the toe of the shoe and eyelets and a new tongue added as before (see Fig. 111).

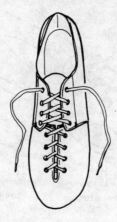

Fig. 111. Extension of lacing in a Gibson style of shoe

This adaptation also makes it easier for a swollen foot to be fitted into the shoe; the fact that the ability to adjust its girth is increased is important, as sometimes a foot swells intermittently; for example it may swell as the day progresses or after a long walk. In this case, some form of expandable footwear is necessary to allow for the difference in size between the morning and the evening.

Another way of extending the opening of the shoe is to have a zip inserted down its full length. A zip may be easier to do up than a lace especially if a ring is added to the zip pull, but this fastening is not adjustable. Again, this adaptation is more easily done to an Oxford style of lacing but other shoes can be adapted if necessary. With boots, it is possible to have a zip down the back to the base of the heel or down the side curving to the forefoot.

Inserting elastic gussets down the sides of shoes will also allow them to be expanded and make them easier to put on. Elastic gussets should not be used if there is instability at the ankle as the elastic allows the foots to twist easily.

To make fastening easier

Lacing adaptations, including those associated with the problems of those people who can only use one hand, are discussed in greater detail in Chapter 10. Those discussed here will need the expertise of an orthopaedic appliance maker or shoe repairer.

One method of adapting laces is to change the closure to a velcro fastening. The hooked section of velcro is attached to one side of the shoe and straps made of the looped section are attached to the other (see Fig. 112). The shoe is then fastened simply by touching the two sides together. This type of fastening can be made stronger by converting it to a cinch fastening; a D-ring is attached to one side of the shoe and straps – made partly of velcro hooks and partly of loops – are attached to the other. The shoe is fastened by passing the strap through the D-ring and touching the two sides of velcro together. Velcro cinch fastenings can also be used to adapt buckle shoes by replacing the buckle with a D-ring.

Velcro makes the fastening infinitely adjustable, and it is strong enough provided it is kept free from dust and particles of clothing. Regular brushing with an old, stiff toothbrush and keeping the hooked velcro covered by the looped (softer) part when the shoes are not being worn will ensure that the velcro is kept clean.

Lace eyelets (unless too large) can easily be replaced by ski-boot hooks to make lacing easier. Special ski-boot, adjustable clip fastenings can also be used.

Fig. 112. Bar and buckle shoe adapted with velcro

Shoes suitable for adaptation

When a shoe adaptation is prescribed, the orthotist will have to decide if it can be carried out on existing footwear or if new shoes must be purchased. If new shoes are required, he will indicate the type of shoe that will be most suitable. Some of the features to look for are shown in Figure 113. If in doubt, the shop assistant should be asked if the shoe can be taken to the hospital for approval. Most shops will allow the shoes to be exchanged if they have not been worn.

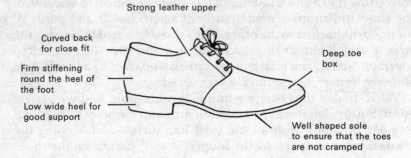

Fig. 113. Suitable shoe for adaptation

The shoe must fit well and hold the foot firmly, gripping the heel. The shoe should also be sturdy, since any adaptation for which it was not designed, will put a strain on it. Tough uppers are essential and leather has been found to withstand adaptation better than man-made materials. The sole should be as durable as possible to withstand the abnormal strain put on it.

The ability to perform adaptations such as shoe raises or inserting caliper sockets will be affected by the type of sole/heel construction of the shoe.

Shoes with separate soles and heels These are suitable for both adaptations. A caliper socket can only be fitted satisfactorily into a solid heel. Shoes which have hollow heels (to reduce the weight) can easily have the heel replaced with a solid one.

Shoes with pre-formed, stuck-on soles A raise can be applied although it may be stuck between the shoe and the sole.

Sockets cannot be inserted in these shoes since they usually have a hollow heel to reduce the weight of the shoe, and new heels cannot be fitted as described above.

Shoes with the sole and heel moulded directly onto them A shoe raise can be applied to these shoes.

They can be fitted with sockets as the heels are solid. (A cut is made in the heel into which the socket is fitted).

Adaptations to shoes for odd sized feet

Many people have feet that are slightly different in size but, if this difference is measurable, it is advisable not to ignore it. Compromise between the two sizes is the worst solution. The larger foot will be cramped into too small an area and the smaller foot will be moving around the shoe at each step.

If the difference is small (½ to 1 size), sometimes wearing lace-up or bar shoes can solve the problem. In the case of the bar, for example, extra holes can be punched in the strap of the shoe of the smaller foot.

If the difference is between 1 and 2 sizes, certain measures can be taken to avoid buying odd shoes.

Padding the tongue (see Fig. 114)

The easiest way of overcoming the problem is to place a pad of adhesive felt (chiropody felt) under the tongue. This will ensure that the foot is kept back in the heel of the shoe (see page 99). The space in the toe portion will be slightly larger than usual but as the toes are prevented from coming forward into this space by the lace and pad, it has no harmful effect.

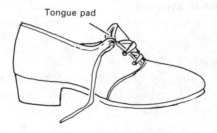

Tongue pad

Fig. 114. Padding the tongue

Insoles

An insole inside a shoe can make the shoe approximately half a size smaller depending on its thickness. The only disadvantage of this method is that the toes may be crushed as there will be less depth in the shoe.

Toe-filler insole   If the difference is only in length, a toe-filler insole can be prescribed. This consists of a thin insole with a covered pad to fit the space between the toes and the end of the shoe. Even though this insole is thin, it is often more comfortable to wear a pair of insoles only one of which has the toe filler.

There is a danger that the toe filler will press on the tips of the toes as the shoe is bent in walking, so the size of the filler must always be considerably smaller than the gap. And the foot must be held firmly so that it does not slide forward in the shoe.

If the difference is more than 2 sizes, shoes of different sizes should be bought (see page 104), although it is sometimes possible to provide satisfactory foam inserts to accommodate the small foot in the shoe which fits the larger foot. Only specialised orthopaedic shoemakers at certain centres can adapt a shoe in this way (see Appendix II). If the foot is very short, the flexible section in the forepart of the shoe will be wrongly positioned and some stiffening of the base will be necessary. A toe block to fill out the inside of the toe will also be required. Similar inserts can be made if the foot (or feet) are very narrow and some of the bones are missing (i.e. absent rays).

This method has the obvious advantage that the insert can be put into different shoes and the added expense of having to obtain odd or special shoes is avoided.

10

Practical Problems

Basic footcare

Basic footcare is essential to healthy, painfree feet and should be as much a part of daily hygiene as combing the hair or brushing the teeth.

Washing the feet daily is important because they are warm and moist and usually kept covered – ideal conditions for bacteria. When the feet are washed the water should be warm 40°C (105°F), and the temperature should be checked before the feet are put in. This temperature will feel warm to the hand or elbow. A thermometer should be used by anyone with diminished sensation in the hands or feet. The soap should be mild to avoid irritation and must be rinsed off carefully.

Drying should be thorough – a soft, absorbant towel used to dab between the toes is recommended but kitchen paper or tissues are highly absorbant and can be very useful. A light dusting of talcum powder may be used to absorb any residual moisture but, if the skin is very dry, it is better to rub in some simple cream.

Any procedure which may damage the skin with the subsequent risk of an infection must be strongly discouraged. These include:

use of sharp instruments to clean round the edges of nails – a nailbrush will be just as effective;

vigorous rubbing as this can damage the skin;

forced separation of the toes when drying.

Soaking the feet for too long can also damage them by decreasing the natural oils in the skin.

Routine footcare is difficult for those who find it difficult to reach their feet. However, there are ways of solving this problem. For example, a shaped piece of flannel or a sponge can be attached to a long handle to extend the reach or a back scrubber can be used. Many back scrubbers have a shaped long handle ideal for reaching the feet; one has velcro hooks on the face onto which can be stuck special slightly abrasive sponges (see Fig. 115). The soft part designed for back scrubbing can be replaced by a slightly tougher (shaped) one for dealing with thickened skin on the sole.

Fig. 115. Washing the foot with an aid

Thickened skin

Thickened skin on the soles and around the margin of the heel acts as a protective layer. It should not be removed unless it is painful or becomes excessively thick.

If the area is rough and damages stockings or socks, it can be smoothed away by gently rubbing with a pumice stone or chiropody sponge when wet (after bathing). No attempt should be made to remove such skin but merely to smooth it. If further measures are necessary, for example if it becomes excessively thick, painful or cracked, a visit to the chiropodist should be advised.

Footcare tips for those with *problem* feet

Some people, such as those with a **diabetic neuropathy** or **poor circulation** in their feet, need to take extra care of their feet. Precautions must be taken to avoid either accidental injury or anything that might reduce the circulation. The following list outlines the major precautions which should be taken by anyone with impaired sensation or diminished circulation in the feet.

1. Feet should be inspected daily for signs of corns, callosities or pressure from stones in shoes or darns in stockings (the inside of shoes should be inspected too).

2. Accidental injury must be guarded against. One way of reducing the risk of injury is never to go barefoot, for example shoes should be kept near the bed at night. Another way is to avoid direct heat sources like hot water bottles which can cause burns if sensation is impaired.

3. If the nails are thickened and hard to cut or eyesight has been impaired by the diabetes, the advice of a chiropodist should be sought.

4. Proprietary preparations should never be used for treatment of corns and callosities. These can contain acid which may burn the skin. A chiropodist should be consulted for treatment of all these conditions.

5. The temperature of the bath water should be tested to avoid scalding. 40°C (105°F) is the maximum temperature for the water and thermometer should always be used if sensation is impaired.

6. Clean hosiery should be put on every day.

7. Extra care should be taken when wearing new shoes which may be stiff at first; for example wearing them only for short periods at the start.

8. Garters, stockings or socks with tight elastic tops should never be worn as these can cut down circulation to the feet; sitting with the legs crossed should be avoided for the same reason.

9. Cold feet should never be allowed to heat up too quickly or get too hot as the peripheral circulation may not be capable of coping immediately with the increased oxygen demand of the worn tissues, and tissue damage can occur.

Danger signs to be watched for

1. Changes in skin colour of the foot or leg.
2. Discharge from under a toenail, corn or crack in the skin.
3. Swelling or throbbing.
4. Severe itching or numbness.

People who need to take extra care of their feet should be encouraged to seek medical advice if any of these signs are noticed.

Nail cutting

Correct cutting of nails is important to prevent painful nail conditions like ingrowing toenails (see page 21).

If the nails are difficult to cut, it may be helpful to advise cutting after a bath or foot wash when the nails are softer.

The correct length of the nail is to just below the tip of the toe (see Fig. 116). Nials cut too short can be very uncomfortable as the soft tissue may bulge around the edge of the nail. Many textbooks advise cutting the toenails straight across but, in practise, this may leave sharp corners which can catch on hosiery and dig into other toes. It is better to advise that the nails are cut slightly curved by following the shape of the end of the toe.

Cutting down the side of the nail must be advised against as this may leave splinters which can grow into the flesh causing infection (see page 21). Attempting to clean the sides of the nail with sharp instruments should also be discouraged as this too can cause infection. Scrubbing with a nailbrush can be just as effective.

Elderly people, who may have been less careful when younger, should be reminded that these procedures need care when circulation is dimished and resistance to infection lower in later life.

Fig. 116. Correct toenail cutting

Instruments for cutting nails

The standard equipment for cutting nails is a pair of small nail nippers and an emery board or nail file for smoothing off the edges after cutting (see Fig. 117). The sharp rigid blade of the nippers cuts easily through thickened nails and can be more comfortable than scissors which may put slight traction on a thick nail as it is cut. Scissors are not recommended for this reason and because they are less safe than nippers. An alternative to nippers, which can be used with the left hand as well as the right, is a pair of nail clippers (see Fig. 118).

If slightly thickened nails are difficult to cut, gentle filing of the surface of the nails with an emery board can be suggested to reduce the thickness of the nail before cutting.

People with poor eyesight should be advised to seek help with this aspect of footcare to avoid damage to their feet when using scissors. When no help is available, they can make their nails more comfortable by filing them down to the correct length with an emery board alone.

Positions for safe and easy toenail cutting

When and where the nails are cut is a very personal matter but some people may need advice about the easiest and most comfortable way of doing this.

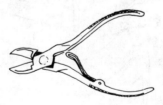

Fig. 117. Nail nippers

Fig. 118. Nail clippers

The body of someone sitting and bending down to the feet on the
floor is unbalanced. Sitting with one leg crossed and the foot
of the crossed leg held straight by the free hand (see Fig. 119) is a
more stable position if there is enough mobility in the hips to adopt
this position. Sitting on a chair immediately in front of the bed with
one foot resting on the bed (see Fig. 119) may be more comfortable
as, although the same degree of bending is needed, some passive
movement is achieved by the pressure of the leg on the bed.

Some people like to stand and rest one foot on a chair. This
position is adequate for someone who is young and has good
balance, but should be discouraged in the older person as the
position is unstable and may result in a fall.

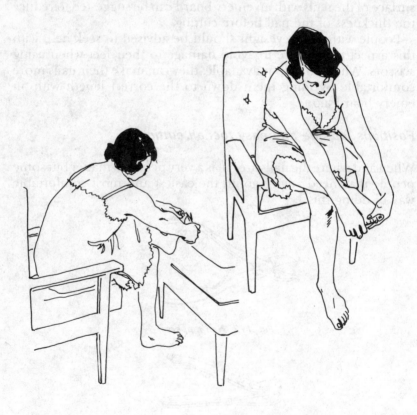

Fig. 119. Positions for easy toenail cutting

Hose

Socks and stockings that are too small can do just as much damage to the feet as shoes that do not fit, so people must be reminded to buy socks of the correct length and ensure they do not shrink (see page 151). Hose sizes are shown on the shoe size chart (see Fig. 77).

Shoe sizes printed on the label of stretch socks can be misleading. They indicate the size from unstretched to fully stretched. When fully stretched, they will exert pressure on the foot, in particular on the toes, which can be harmful. Hose worn as tight as this can also make the feet cold by eliminating the trapped air in the fibres which usually insulates the foot. They will also be much harder to get on and off. It is advisable therefore to buy socks whose unstretched (first) size corresponds to the size of the foot. For example, when sizes range from 1 to 3 and 4 to 7, someone with size 2 feet should buy the larger size.

A wide range of types of hose is currently available, ranging from hold-up stockings to body-free tights, each with their own specific application.

Stockings The suspenders needed to hold up stockings can be awkward for stiff or disabled fingers. If the suspenders are detached from the belt or garment they can be fastened to the sockings without any tension and be hooked, buttoned or attached with velcro to the belt, etc. Other alternatives may be more practical.

Tights These need no suspenders but some people find them difficult to pull on and off and get very hot in them. They are available in a large range of sizes though many are made in one size. Other possibilities are: open-crotch tights (tights which are not sewn together between the legs); body-free tights (tights with holes in the front/back and sides for coolness); Tytex stocking tights (separate legs each with a waistband).

Hold-ups (stockings which are held up by elasticated fabric or a band of rubbery material inside the top edge). The main advantage of these stockings is that no suspenders are needed but care must be taken to ensure that the tops are not too tight as they could then diminish the circulation to the leg. They also have no heel shaping which can make them easier to get on.

Pop-socks (stockings to below the knee held up by elastic at the top). These are ideal under trousers and are made by many manufacturers. Those with a wide band of elastic round the top can be more comfortable; again, these socks should not be too tight. They also have no heel shaping.

Above-knee socks   These have shaped feet, are made in a variety of fibres – wool, acrylic and mixtures – and are usually thick and warm.

Heel-less socks (socks without heel shaping). These socks, which can be knitted at home (a pattern is available from the Disabled Living Foundation, see Appendix II for address) can be pulled on quickly (without the wearer having to make sure which is the front or back). Those who find it difficult to reach down to their feet or who are confused will therefore find these socks useful. They may wrinkle excessively over the front of the ankle so should not be worn by those with insensitive feet in case the shoe presses on a wrinkle causing a sore.

Most socks have elastic in the top. This can be uncomfortable for people with swollen ankles or varicose veins and may cause superficial skin damage. However, some men's socks are available without elastic. Some firms and organisations are willing to knit hose to measure for people with difficult feet.

The blends of fibres used in hose are varied, ranging from pure wool or cotton (lisle) and mixtures containing wool or cotton together with synthetic fibres, to those which are entirely man-made such as rayon and nylon.

Some people are unable to wear synthetic materials and will need to wear hose made from natural materials. Those with skin conditions like eczema may find cotton hose more comfortable and a list of suppliers can be obtained from the Disabled Living Foundation (see Appendix II). Nylon stockings are also available with cotton underfoot and in the crotch gusset.

Much hose is made of a mixture of synthetic and natural substances to combine the comfort of natural fibres with the hard wearing qualities of synthetics. Mixtures have another advantage pertinent to foot health which is not often recognised. They help to transfer moisture away from the skin (wicking). It is important that the foot is not constantly in a moist environment (see page 28) but, as the foot has a greater number of sweat glands than any other part

of the body, this can be difficult to achieve. Natural fibres will
absorb this moisture and keep the foot dry but this moisture
remains in the material which, when saturated, will present a wet
surface to the skin. Synthetic fibres on the other hand absorb very
little moisture but, provided there is an absorbant surface on the
other side – for example a leather upper – they will allow moisture
to pass through. This process is known as wicking. Hose made of
man-made fibres or mixtures are therefore more likely to keep the
skin surface dry and healthy than purely natural fibres as long as
there is an absorbant material in the shoe. Shoes made and/or lined
in synthetic materials will not absorb the moisture, wicking will not
take place and the moisture will stay on the skin which, ultimately,
will become 'soggy'.

Care of hose

One of the problems inherent in hose is that it can shrink and, as
has already been said, hose that is too small can damage feet and
restrict circulation. Materials made of natural fibres are known to
shrink but synthetic fibres can shrink also – the amount being
governed by the way the fibres are knitted. Garments undergo
rigorous testing before being mass-produced and the care label will
give instructions to suit the combination of the material and the way
it was knitted. Unlike clothes, in which the label is sewn into the
garment, the instructions on socks and stockings usually appear on
the package or on an adhesive label (see Fig. 120) which is removed
before wearing. Noting down and following these instructions will
ensure longer lasting, better fitting hose. *Note:* when fibre content
only is shown on the label, washing instructions can be found from
information on the side of washing powder packets.

Fig. 120. Care label in hose

Putting on hose

Anyone who has difficulty in reaching down to his feet will find it difficult to put on hose. The standard sock gutter (see Fig. 121) is probably the best known aid to overcome this problem but it can be awkward to manage at first and needs careful instruction. Sometimes getting the sock or stocking onto the aid is difficult. If so, holding the gutter between the knees can make it easier to manoeuvre the stocking into place with either a single hand or both.

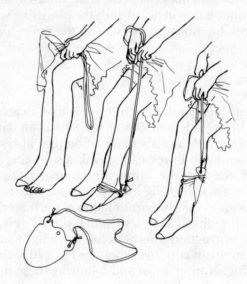

Fig. 121. Use of a sock/stocking gutter

Storing the gutter rolled up with an elastic band round it will also make it easier to get the stocking on, as this will ensure that the gutter remains curled.

The size of the gutter is important too as, if it is too big, it may be hard to manoeuvre around the ankle. Standard plastic shapes may need to be cut down to fit. The problem caused by the plastic sticking to the foot can be overcome by either sprinkling a little talcum powder on to the gutter before use or sticking a square of material to the inside of the gutter. The length of the tapes is also important as, if they are too long, not enough leverage will be applied.

To help in putting on tights, a double gutter is available. Stockists of aids are listed in Appendix II.

Elastic stockings are difficult to put on using a gutter as a more rigid gutter would be needed for this, but getting the stocking on to the gutter may then prove too difficult. A floor standing aid with a robust metal frame has been designed to help with support stockings. Both hands are free to put the stocking on the aid although this may still be difficult.

Many aids exist to help patients having difficulty with a particular sock or stocking aid. The one shown in Figure 122 – the Neatfeat aid – can be used by someone who is one-handed. The wide basket on which the stocking is pulled enables the whole foot to be inserted in one movement before the aid is pulled up the leg. Tights can be brought to knee-level one at a time, then pulled up conventionally.

Another aid which can be used with one hand, the Brevetti, is seen in Figure 123, although someone with the use of only one hand may find it hard to get the stocking onto it. This aid has two functions – the bucket-shaped end is used in the same manner as the Neatfeat aid to put on stockings or tights and the other end acts as a long-handled shoe horn. The shoe horn also has a dual role with a notch which can be used to help remove the hose (see Fig. 123).

Fig. 122. Use of the Neatfeat aid

Taking off hose can be just as difficult as putting it on, although there are fewer commercially available aids. A long-handled shoe horn can be adapted to act as an effective stocking remover by attaching a small plastic flange to the back of the shoe

horn. The tip of the horn is slipped into the top of the stocking and
the flange pushes it down.

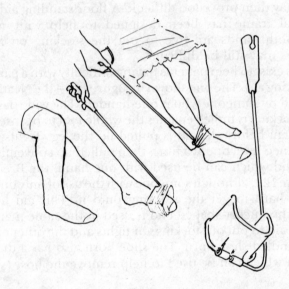

Fig. 123. Use of the Brevetti aid to put on and take off socks/stockings

Sometimes an aid is not the answer to problems encountered
when putting on hose. All that may be required is advice on a
suitable dressing position. Sitting in a safe, balanced position in
which muscle power and joint range can be used to their best
advantage may make the task easier. Sitting with the legs crossed can
be helpful. The chair must be the correct height so that one foot can
be rested flat on the floor and, if possible, should have arms. If the
hose is carefully folded before it is put on, only one hand will be
needed to stretch down to the top of the toes to slip it on – an extra
saving in energy (see Fig. 124).

Socks and stockings are often put on standing with one foot in the
air, but, trying to do this when balance is impaired, can lead to falls.
However, standing to put on hose can be made safer if the foot is
rested on a stool or chair placed near a wall or solid piece of
furniture like a bed end.

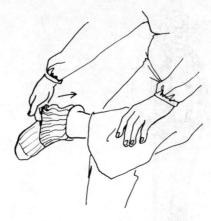

Fig. 124. Sitting to put on socks

Keeping warm

Keeping the feet and legs warm is very important particularly if the circulation is impaired or mobility is limited. Woollen hose is warm and comfortable because the wool fibres naturally trap air (an excellent insulator). However, hose made from other fibres will be equally warm if it is knitted so that the maximum amount of air is trapped and/or has a raised pile surface which also holds air.

Those who sit for long periods or whose circulation to the legs is impaired have to make a conscious effort to keep warm. Elderly people may have the added problem of impaired sensation.

It must be remembered that heat can best be conserved if the whole leg, rather than just the feet, is kept warm. Grannies may not relish the thought of wearing 'jeans' (see Fig. 125) but trousers certainly keep the legs warm, as do thick stockings/socks and leg warmers!

Slippers with a sheepskin or artificial fleece lining will be warm as an insulating layer of air is trapped in the fleece. If the slipper is too small, the fleece will be compressed and the amount of air will be reduced; the slipper is then no warmer than any other. Bootee style slippers, covering a slightly greater area, are also warm.

Keeping the feet warm can be a particular problem for people sitting in wheelchairs; they must be encouraged to put their feet up for short periods each day (see page 54) to maintain good

Fig. 125. 'Grannies in jeans'

circulation in their feet; they should also be encouraged to wear
warm footwear, for example, slipper sox or sheepskin boots (see
Fig. 126); trousers, quilted trousers and leg warmers can also be
helpful. A foot muff can be a 'warm' solution for those who cannot
stand to transfer. The lined quilted wheelchair 'leg bags', up to the
waist, can give excellent protection inside the house and out of
doors.

Fig. 126. Sheepskin boots

Sitting next to a heat source like a fire or a radiator should be discouraged as poor skin sensation can lead to burns. For a similar reason, hot water bottles should not be used. Once feet are cold, they should not be warmed up too quickly; tissue damage may occur if the peripheral circulation cannot cope immediately with the increased oxygen demand of the warm tissue.

An electric under- or over-blanket to pre-warm the bed is an ideal way of ensuring warm feet at night. Hot water bottles can also be used to pre-warm the bed, but they should be filled very carefully to avoid accidents. They are easier to handle if covered, and should be taken out of the bed before it is slept in. Bedsocks are also excellent foot warmers as long as they are not held on tightly by a band around the ankle as this may diminish the circulation to the feet. Warming the feet before getting into bed, for example in a warm bath or a foot bath, may help; failing that, up and down movements of the ankle may improve the blood circulating to the feet which will help to warm them.

Special 'socks' are available for wearing inside outdoor boots. Wearing two pairs of socks is another way of increasing the number of insulating layers, but the outer pair must be a size bigger than the inner and the shoes and boots large enough to accommodate the extra socks or, again, the insulating layer of air will be lost.

Warm insoles inside shoes will also help maintain foot heat. Patients may need reminding that, if they are using a thick, furry insole, the shoe must be deep enough to ensure that the foot is not compressed. Some thermal insoles have a silvery surface which acts by reflecting the body heat back to the foot. None of these products will actually warm the feet – they will only maintain the heat already present. Pre-warming the feet before putting on the hose and shoes is a good habit to encourage (see page 27), as is pre-warming socks and shoes – perhaps by putting them in an airing cupboard.

Care of shoes

Shoes should be changed regularly; this is most important if feet are to remain healthy. Wearing one pair of shoes continuously is not very healthy, since the shoe will absorb a certain amount of moisture each day which needs time to dry out, but people with awkward feet, who may have only one pair of outdoor shoes that fit, should be advised to change into an indoor pair when at home to give their outdoor shoes as long as possible to dry out.

Changing shoes regularly will keep the ankle and foot supple if the heels vary in height. However, elderly people who have worn shoes with the same heel height for many years, should not be advised to change this practice since their balance mechanisms will be set to the one height (see page 100).

Care of the outside of shoes will depend on the materials from which the shoes are made. For example, leather uppers should be polished regularly to feed the leather and keep it supple and more resistant to water. Regular checks on the state of repair of the shoe, particularly the soles, are important as worn heels can cause instability.

Wear in other places will also need attention. An awkward walking pattern can cause wear to the toes of the shoes. Additional toecaps can be made out of a number of materials, for example rubber or plastic, and fitting can be arranged by an orthotist. Two do-it-yourself applications of toe capping material are available (see Appendix II for suppliers).

Putting on shoes

A pair of shoes which seemed perfectly comfortable in the shop when being tried on may seem to fit less well when they have been purchased and brought home. There may be a number of reasons for this. First, the feet may be more swollen than they were in the shop; trying the shoes on again the following morning will establish whether this was in fact the cause. Secondly, the way in which the shoes are put on may affect the fit. In the shoe shop, the shoes are put on and fastened while the foot is resting on a sloping board with a ledge to support the heel. This is the best possible position in which to put on shoes, as the weight is on the back of the heel ensuring that it is right back in the heel of the shoe while the laces are being done up. When putting shoes on at home, people tend just to slip their feet in and lace the shoes up and, if the heel is not as far back in the shoe as it was in the shop, the shoes will appear uncomfortable. People should therefore be advised to lace up their shoes while sitting with the foot resting on a chair or a stool with the weight on the back of the heel.

Fastening adaptations

Being able to tie one's own shoe laces is an important part of independent living. However, this is an activity which many people find difficult mainly because they are unable to reach their own feet due to stiff joints or because they are unable to use one hand following a stroke. Several simple methods of adapting the lacing on shoes can make it possible for these people to regain complete independence, although careful teaching and encouragement will be necessary before they can master the new methods.

For all these adaptations, a longer lace than the type usually supplied will be needed. If the correct length is not available, strong string or stool cord can be used as a substitute.

Dressing-stick method

This method is suitable both for those who are unable to reach down to their feet to do up their laces, and for those with the use of only one hand.

A knot is tied in one end of the lace which is threaded as shown in Figure 127. A loop is made in the free end of the lace and a piece of the looped side of velcro is sewn on to the base of this. An equivalent hooked portion of velcro is sewn onto the outside of the shoe as shown. Hooking the dressing stick through a hole punched in the top of the tongue will prevent it rucking when the foot is inserted in the shoe and also stops the shoe moving.

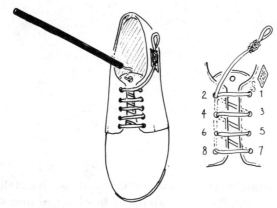

Fig. 127. Adapted lacing – dressing-stick method

The lace is tightened by pulling with the dressing stick on the top loop, then on the next one down, and so on until the loop at the bottom of the lace is tightened. The free end of the lace is then pulled in and fixed by pressing the two portions of velcro together. To loosen the lacing, the process is reversed. It sometimes helps if small loops are attached to the back of the shoe heel so that these can be held by the dressing stick when putting the foot into the shoe to stop the back of the heel folding in.

One-handed method

The next two methods are also suitable for those who cannot use both hands.

A knot is tied in one end of the lace as in the dressing-stick method. The way it is threaded is also similar (see Fig. 128), the only difference being that when the threading is completed, the lace is passed down through the last bottom eyelet and through a hole punched in the tongue and then comes up through a similar hole under the top eyelet on that side.

The lace is tightened from the top loop downwards and the end of the lace is fixed by looping it through the top of the lacing as shown in the Figure. The tongue is stopped from being pushed down into the shoe as the foot is inserted by the lacing passing through the tongue. The lace is loosened by undoing the loop in the lace and loosening from the bottom.

Fig. 128. Adapted lacing — one-handed lace

One-handed hook method

Ski-boot hooks are sometimes easier to manage with one hand than traditional lacing and small eyelets can easily be changed into ski-boot hooks.

Again, a knot is tied in one end of the lace but this time it is
threaded from the bottom (see Fig. 129). A ring is attached to the
other end of the lace and, after the lace has been threaded over the
hooks as shown, this can neatly be secured on one of the ski-boot
hooks.

The special clips used on ski boots are also easy to fasten and can
be used by people who can use only one hand. Ordinary lace-up
shoes can be adapted in this way.

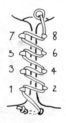

Fig. 129. Adapted fastening – one-handed hook

Other methods

Another method to enable shoes to be laced with one hand
involves pop rivetting a small plastic disc through the top eyelets of
the shoe. The lace is threaded in the normal way but laces are
tightened and fixed by being wound round between the plastic rivet
and the shoe. Round laces should be used for this adaptation.

A small device called 'No-Bows' which enables laces to be
fastened with only one hand is available from aids suppliers (see
Appendix II). To use this method efficiently, considerable manual
dexterity is needed as well as a strong pinch grip as the ends of the
aid are compressed to adjust the lace. The lace is held in place
automatically when the ends are released.

Difficulty in tying laces can also be overcome by changing the
fastening to velcro (see page 139); shoes fastening by this method
are sometimes available commercially (see Fig. 130).

Elastic laces will also solve the problem of tying bows as they will
stretch enough without being untied to allow the shoes to be
slipped on using a shoe horn. Available in a number of different
lengths from aids suppliers (see Appendix II), these laces
effectively convert the shoe into a slip-on type which comes higher

up the instep than a standard casual and so holds the foot more firmly in place (see page 100). The main disadvantage of this adaption is that the laces tend to wear out quickly, but if they are used double or strong four-cord elastic reinforced at the ends by glue is used instead, they can help the user to become independent. If elastic lacing is used, the tongue should be stitched to the shoe down one side to prevent it rucking as the foot is pushed in, or the lace threaded through the tongue on one side at the top of the lacing as previously suggested (see page 160).

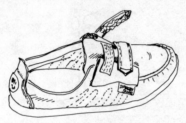

Fig. 130. Shoe fastened with velcro

Buckles can be difficult to manage also. If so, they can be removed and sewn on again attached to a piece of doubled strong elastic. When the buckle is fastened, the shoe is converted into a slip-on and a shoe horn will be needed to ease the shoe on to the foot. The buckle can also be removed and the fastening converted to a velcro cinch fastening (see page 160).

Shoe aids

A shoe horn, which can be used to ease the shoe on and prevent the back of the shoe wearing down, should always be used when casual shoes or shoes which have been adapted to slip on are worn.

For those who find it difficult to bend, a standard shoe horn may not be long enough. It can be extended simply with a length of dowel rod but long-handled shoe horns are available from aids suppliers in a variety of different lengths (see Fig. 131). Some also have a flexible section to make it easier for the foot to be slipped into the shoe.

The No-stoop lever (see Fig. 132) has the same function as a long-handled shoe horn but is a much more compact aid. It is fitted on to the shoe before the shoe is lowered to the floor suspended on a cord. It then acts as a shoe horn as the foot is slipped in but, once the shoe is on, the lever can be removed by pulling on the cord. This aid is small enough to fit into a pocket and is therefore useful for patients regularly visiting hospital clinics or physiotherapy departments where they are likely to be asked to remove their shoes.

Fig. 131. Use of long handled shoehorn

Fig. 132. No-stoop lever

Taking off shoes can be just as much of a problem as getting them on. A boot jack (see Fig. 133) can be used to help to remove shoes. The shoe is placed in the notch in the boot jack as shown. Pressing on the top of the boot jack with the other foot ensures that the shoe is kept still while the foot is removed.

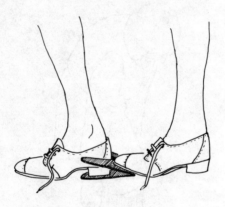

Fig. 133. Boot jack

Slipping, tripping and falling (see Fig. 134)

Ill-fitting footwear can cause people to slip and fall (see page 101), but it is by no means the only cause. Damage sustained during a fall and/or fear of falling after an accident are factors which can severely limit mobility. This subject is, therefore, of great importance to disabled and elderly people.

Home visits to elderly people whose mobility is impaired or who are worried about the possibility of falls will often reveal a number of obvious hazards such as loose rugs on a lino floor, a trailing electric flex or a poorly-lit staircase. Unfortunately, the removal of such things, while creating a safer environment, may not help to increase the old person's confidence and a deeper study of the problem will be needed.

The following section lists some of the factors that can lead to instability which, when explained, may help to boost confidence.

Fig. 134. 'Avoiding slips'

General points about stability

1. A person is more stable when wearing shoes than when barefoot.

2. A short person is more stable than a tall person.

3. A person is less stable when carrying something – women being slightly more affected by this than men.

4. The higher the heel worn, the less stable the wearer will be.

Falls in the home

Falls often occur soon after someone gets up from a rest because the cerebral circulation is unable to adjust quickly enough. People should be advised to change their position slowly and wait a few moments after getting up before starting to walk. If conditions are slippery out of doors, they should take the extra precaution of walking around indoors before going out.

Falls can also be associated with sudden neck movements particularly looking upwards suddenly. It is for this reason that elderly people often fall when hanging out washing, putting up curtains or reaching up to a shelf.

It is known that falls occur more frequently later in the day when people are beginning to tire, so people worried about falling should be advised to go out in the morning.

Instability can be caused by changing footwear, for example changing from slippers to heavier outdoor shoes or boots. Another useful tip, therefore, is that a short gentle walk indoors after changing shoes will allow time for the balance mechanisms to adapt to the weight of new footwear.

Getting out of bed at night is another danger period, particularly if the person involved is used to wearing high heels. Because the balance mechanisms of the elderly woman will be set for the high heel, she will tend to lean back excessively when walking in low heels or barefoot so that she is unstable. If this is the case, barefoot walking should be avoided and footwear should be kept close to the bed or, if the reason for getting up in the night is the need to go to the lavatory or, possibly, to make a phone call, a commode or a telephone should be placed as near as possible to the bedside.

Stairs are another danger area. More falls occur coming down than going up, particularly on stairs which turn corners and on which the tread is diminished. Good, even lighting is important in all areas but special attention should be paid to the stairs. People who wear bifocals may have difficulty in seeing the treads of the stairs as they descend; if this is a real problem, their glasses could be made up to a different prescription (the bottom part of the lens to focus at a greater distance). If this is done, anyone reading a book would have to hold it further away but seeing to descend the stairs would be easier.

Falls when carrying

Carrying objects, particularly large or heavy ones, is known to precipitate falls, so it is important to warn people to take care when carrying anything. The fact that the arm swing, very important to normal walking, is restricted when carrying accounts for the decrease in stability. The ability of this swing to lessen the rotary force of the trunk is lost when someone is walking and carrying an object with both hands; when walking and carrying things with one hand, the rotation force tends to make the swinging leg swing in just before the foot is put down which can lead to instability.

Large objects, which can block a person's view of the ground immediately in front of him, and so impair his balance, cause greater problems than small objects. Heavy objects can also cause someone to slip since the instinctive reaction of the carrier is to move faster than usual in order to get the objects to their destination more quickly.

When walking, the eyes gauge distance from objects along the way. However, the head of someone who limps, moves up and down at each step so that this information can be distorted and lead to instability. People who cannot walk without limping should be warned to walk more slowly.

Footwear

Footwear is an obvious culprit. Some soles are more slippery than others (see page 90) but a non-slip tread is important. All shoe soles including slippers need to be checked for signs of wear as worn-away heels can make the wearer very unstable and some slipper soles can become shiny with use (the same applies to the rubber ferrules on walking sticks and crutches).

Slippery conditions

The snow and ice encountered in winter can make walking very hazardous. Some people, particularly those who have had a fall in similar conditions, may be scared to venture out. One simple piece of advice to such people is that they should take shorter steps and move slowly to decrease the likelihood of slipping.

To combat treacherous conditions or to give extra confidence, several types of anti-slip device can be pulled on over a pair of walking shoes to provide a spiked or chained walking surface (see Fig. 135) (see Appendix II for suppliers).

For those who find it difficult to reach the public highway in freezing conditions, a heated non-slip surface can be put down which will melt the covering of snow or ice. This is particularly useful on ramps.

Another useful aid is a walking stick with a metal point on it enabling the user to get better purchase on ice and snow, but this would involve buying a special stick for icy weather. One company markets a metal walking stick with a rubber ferrule out of which a

tungsten carbide point can be extended for use in icy conditions
(see Fig. 136). It may also be possible to use a shooting stick with a
spike; such a stick has the added advantage of a handle which opens
out into a seat.

Fig. 135. Non-slip device

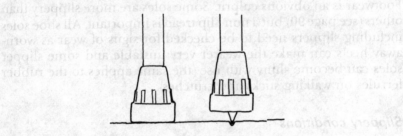

Fig. 136. Screw-on tip for a walking stick

Posture

Feet held in any position for a long period of time will tend to stiffen
into this position. Examples of this are curled toes due to short
hose or shoes and shortening of the achilles tendon due to
wearing high heels. For this reason, any habitual posture should be
guarded against.

Chairs which are the correct height are most important (see
page 51). If the seat is too high, the feet will hang down unsupported
and there will be extra pressure on the backs of the legs. If too low,
the whole posture is affected and the feet can be placed in awkward
positions.

Sleeping positions should be noted too. One position adopted
regularly, particularly by those on sedation who do not move as

much in their sleep, may lead to a deformity. One example of this is lying on one's side in bed with the top leg resting on the bed as seen in Figure 137. The big toe is being pushed inwards into a *valgus* position and this may exaggerate a deformity in someone who is prone to it.

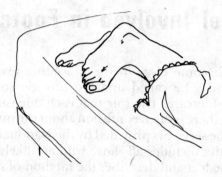

Fig. 137. Poor foot position in bed

Appendix I

Personnel Involved in Footcare

As will have become clear in the preceding text, a number of professionals may be called upon to provide solutions for foot problems and footcare. The role that each one can play has been described, but there is often confusion about the method of referral and whether the service is provided by the National Health Service.

This appendix includes all those who are likely to be involved with care of the feet and describes the method of referral to them. Broadly they can be divided into two groups: those who can treat patients without referral from a registered medical practitioner or health clinic and those who cannot.

Those who do not need referral

Chiropodist

Chiropodists are specialists in foot health maintenance. The training lasts three years leading to eligibility for membership of the Society of Chiropodists (MChS) and State Registration (SRCh). Only state registered chiropodists are employed by the National Health Service.

Chiropody services are provided by the National Health Service with priority for:

children at school or of pre-school age;

expectant mothers;

registered disabled people;

old age pensioners.

People with medical conditions outside these groups may be accepted subject to current limitation of resources.

The services are available through hospitals, health centres, clinics, occasionally mobile clinics and a domiciliary service for those who are housebound. Some districts arrange transport for patients. Some centres have chiropody (foot care) .assistants who work under the supervision of trained chiropodists.

Chiropody can also be obtained through private practitioners. Information about State Registered Chiropodists in particular areas can be obtained from the Society of Chiropodists and copies of the Chiropodists' Register are kept in public libraries.

Foot care assistant

Foot care assistants are employed predominantly within the National Health Service to act as a clinical aid to state registered chiropodists. One of their functions is to provide simple foot care and hygiene to patients under the supervision of a chiropodist. Their role is not one of treatment but one of care involving simple toe-nail cutting, rubbing in cream and often footwear advice.

Toe-nail cutter

Toe-nail cutting services, operated on a voluntary basis are available in some areas. These may or may not be in co-operation with district chiropody services. Where possible volunteers receive initial training from the local chiropodist and only carry out procedures which the person would normally do for themselves (washing and toe-nail cutting).

These services are operated by members of Age Concern and the British Red Cross Society and are provided free or for a small contribution to funds. Most sessions are held once a month in old peoples' homes or day centres, for old or disabled people no longer able to cope with their own foot care but not in need of chiropody.

In the areas where services exist anyone can ask for someone to receive this type of foot care.

Shoe fitter

There are no compulsory qualifications for working as a shoe fitter. Shops which employ trained staff usually display their certificates in the shop. Fitters can receive training in several ways.

1. By passing an examination held by the Society of Shoe Fitters to qualify for membership of the Society of Shoe Fitters (ASSDF). Preparation for the examination can be by a correspondence course or in-shop training.

2. Attending a course held by a manufacturer or trade association (for example, Clark's).

3. Receiving in-service training from an experienced fitter on the staff.

Addresses of shops with trained fitters can be obtained from the Society of Shoe Fitters.

Shoe shops which are members of the Children's Foot Health Register agree to have staff who have been trained in one of the above ways or who have had five years' experience in fitting children's shoes. They also agree to stock children's shoes and sandals in four width fittings in whole and half sizes from infants size 4½ to adults size 6. There is no similar register currently available for adult footwear.

Those who need referral from a Registered Medical Practitioner

Physiotherapist

Physiotherapists are specialists in rehabilitation using physical methods. The training lasts three years leading to membership of the Chartered Society of Physiotherapy (MCSP). Members can apply for State Registration (SRP) and only state registered physiotherapists (a list of which is kept by the Council for Professions Supplementary to Medicine) are employed by the National Health Service.

All those who need physiotherapy are eligible for treatment through the National Health Service. Services are normall co-ordinated for the district health authority by the district physio-therapist, and are given on an out-patient or in-patient basis. A domiciliary service may sometimes be provided where appropriate.

Physiotherapy is also available from private practitioners. Information about private practitioners in particular areas can be obtained from the Chartered Society of Physiotherapists and copies of the *Physiotherapists' Register* are kept in public libraries.

Occupational therapist

Occupational therapists are specialists in rehabilitation, the emphasis in their work being on daily living activities and independence in self care. Successful completion of their three-year training leads to a Diploma of the College of Occupational Therapy (DipCOT). Only state registered occupational therapists are employed by the National Health Service. A list is kept by the Council for Professions Supplementary to Medicine.

Like physiotherapy, occupational therapy is provided by the National Health Service for in- and out-patients attending hospitals and day centres. A service is also provided in the community by social services departments and some occupational therapists are employed by district health departments.

There are few private practitioners and a register of occupational therapists in private practice is held by the Council for Professions Supplementary to Medicine.

Nursing staff

The health visitor is a state registered nurse with further training and qualifications. As a member of the primary health care team she is able to advise on general foot care with emphasis on the preventative aspects. Where further investigation and treatment is required the health visitor can identify and make the appropriate referrals.

The district nurse is also an SRN or SEN with post-basic training and is well placed through her work with elderly people in their own homes to identify, refer or treat the foot problems of patients or of those caring for them. Many district nurses liaise closely with the departments of geriatric medicine or the district general hospital, and many are based in the health centre giving them access to colleagues. Certain advice can be obtained without medical referral.

Geriatric visitors

Geriatric visitors are specialised nurses who have completed a period of in-service training following state registration. The accent of this service is on regular surveillance and thereby prevention of serious problems. It is provided through the local community care service in some (mainly inner city) areas, for all retired women over the age of 60 and all retired men over 65, and is not available privately.

Request for a visit from a geriatric visitor can be made by anyone, but initial enquiry should be directed to the local health centre or clinic which will be able to advise whom to contact.

Orthotist

Orthotists are involved in the design, measurement and application of orthopaedic appliances (orthoses).

Their training lasts for four years leading to the award of a Diploma of Licentiate of the Institute of British Surgical Technologists (LIBST). Other paramedical disciplines within this Institute are prosthetists (artificial limb makers) and dental technicians.

Orthotic service is available from the National Health Service either by hospital-employed orthotic staff, or by orthotists from private companies giving a sub-contracted service to hospitals.

Orthotists in private practice may also be seen without medical referral. The Institute of British Surgical Technologists will supply information about the availability of orthotists in different areas.

Surgical footwear maker

Surgical footwear makers specialise in making or adapting footwear for people with lower limb or foot deformities.

Because of the comparatively small number of companies spread throughout the country, training is usually carried out within the company, and lasts for four to seven years.

Surgical footwear can be obtained through the National Health Service, free of charge, on referral from a registered practitioner attached to a hospital. Assessment and measurement are made by an orthotist and passed to the surgical shoe maker, many surgical footwear makers being qualified orthotists themselves.

Surgical footwear can be obtained privately by direct contact with the maker who will assess, measure and make, no referral being necessary from a medical practitioner.

Appendix II

Sources of Information

MANUFACTURERS/ SUPPLIERS OF READY-MADE ORTHOPAEDIC AND SPECIAL FOOTWEAR MENTIONED IN THE TEXT

Bury Boot & Shoe Co Ltd Brandlesholme Road Bury Lancs BL8 1BG *Tel:* 061 764 5317	Extra special shoes
Camp Ltd 116 Tower Bridge Road London SE1 3NG *Tel:* 01 237 3195 ext 13	The Camp adult shoe and felt boots
AND	
Northern Division 15 Moss Street Liverpool L6 FEY *Tel:* 051 207 1675	
Cooper P. R. (Footline) Ltd Seaford House 27 Stoughton Street South Leicester LE2 0SH *Tel:* 0533 29482	'Mo' shoes and felt boots Cooper 'Kids' boots

Cumbria Orthopaedic Ltd   Soft boots
Floor 6, Shaddon Mills
Carlisle
Cumbria CA2 5TY
Tel: 0228 29774

AND

Cumbria Orthopaedic   Soft boots
(London) Ltd
St Johns Hospital
Morden Hill
Lewisham
London SE13 7NW
Tel: 01 852 9533

Drew John (London) Ltd   The Drushoe
433 Uxbridge Road
Ealing
London W5 3NT
Tel: 01 992 0381

Dudley Surgical Appliances Ltd   The Alpha and Beta boot and
Horseley Heath   shoe and the Rehab canvas,
Tipton   toeless boot and sandal
West Midlands DT4 7AA
Tel: 021 557 4204/7192

Gilbert & Mellish Ltd   Piedro boot
503 Bristol Road   Piedro ladies and gents shoes
Birmingham B29 6AU
Tel: 021 472 0967

Hall, Ken Ltd   Radus shoes
39 Regent Street   Nustyle shoes
Kettering   Felt boots
Northants NN16 8BR   Biffabout boot
Tel: 0536 516674/522468

Kettering Surgical Appliances
Ltd
5 Harlesdon Road
St. James
Northampton NN5 5LH
Tel: 0604 57179

The Multifit shoe
Felt boots
Solidus shoe
Ortho boot

LSB Orthopaedics Ltd
203-4 Melchett Road
Kings Norton Factory Centre
Birmingham B30 3HU
Tel: 021 458 2425

Comfort shoes
Soft shoes
Felt boots
Kickabout boot

Orthopaedic Footwear Co Ltd
(James Taylor & Son Ltd)
4 Paddington Street
Marylebone High Street
London W1M 3LA
Tel: 01 935 4149

Solidus shoe
Surgical boots

Orthopaedic Systems
14 Mersey Road
Widnes
Cheshire WA8 0DS
Tel: 051 709 3232 or
051 420 6409

Vinyl or canvas post-operative
and rehabilitation boots and
sandals

Pryor & Howard Ltd
39 Willow Lane
Mitcham
Surrey CR4 4US
Tel: 01 648 1177

Leather post-operative *Hallux
Valgus* sandal

Remploy Ltd
Medical Products Division
415 Edgeware Road
London NW2 6LR
Tel: 01 452 8020

'Soft' shoes in waterproof
stiffened fabric
Felt boots
Hill boots

NOTE

For information on manufacturers of felt or open-to-toe boots not listed or manufacturers making shoes in extra small/narrow, extra large/wide or extra deep, contact the Clothing Adviser at the Disabled Living Foundation. Please send an SAE for a copy of the Footwear Information List. (Address, see page 187.)

SLIPPERS

Bury Boot & Shoe Co Ltd (See page 175)	A laced boot slipper
Camp Ltd (See page 175)	Zip-to-toe washable boot and shoe-style slipper
Cooper P. R. (Footline) Ltd (See page 175)	Zip-to-toe washable boot and shoe-style slippers
Damart Thermawear (Bradford) Ltd Bowling Green Mills Bingley West Yorkshire BD16 3ZD *Tel:* 0254 558221	Zip-up warm slippers

LOUNGING OR SLIP-ON SLIPPERS

Damart Thermawear (Bradford) Ltd (See above)	Lounging slippers Bed socks
Golden Footprints Ltd Upper Sapey Worcester WR6 6XT	Birkenstock sandals

MADE TO MEASURE FOOTWEAR

Adams & Jones
Crispin Hall
High Street
Street
Somerset BA16 0EZ
Tel: 0458 45441

Moccasin style shoes, boots and sandals made to measure on adapted standard lasts

Coopers P. R. (Footline) Ltd
(See page 175)

Footline shoes made on a plaster cast of the foot

Frank Harvey & Co
Violet Hill Road
Stowmarket
Suffolk IP14 1NE
Tel: 0449 612646

'John Locke' shoes made to measure on adapted standard lasts via retail outlets

Soma UK Ltd
3-7 Moss Street
Liverpool L6 1EY
Tel: 051 207 3534

'John Locke' shoes made to measure on adapted standard lasts for the National Health Service

Wood, John & Son
Linton
Old Cleeve
Minehead
Somerset TA24 6HT
Tel: 0984 40291

Made-to-measure sheepskin bootees

SAFETY AIDS

Davies & Co (Kettering) Ltd
Durban Road
Kettering
Northants NN16 0JW
Tel: 0536 513456

Schuh Spikes

Hopes Mail Order
31-35 Blenheim Gardens
London SW2 5EU
Tel: 01 671 5133

Grippex Snow Chains

Rud Chains Ltd
1-3 Belmont Road
Whitstable
Kent CT5 1QJ
Tel: 0227 266464

'RUD' chains

TEMPORARY FOOTWEAR AND PRESSURE SORE PREVENTION

Brinmark Ltd
Nether Street
London N3 1RL
Tel: 01 349 0135/6

Synthetic sheepskin squares,
heel protectors, etc

Dermalex Co Ltd
146-154 Kilburn High Road
London NW6 4JD
Tel: 01 624 4686

Lambpad slipper (available with
removable rubber sole).
Also make other natural
sheepskin products

Henleys Medical Supplies
Alexandra Works
Clarendon Road
London N8 0DL
Tel: 01 889 3151

Pillow Paws non-slip stretchy
slippers

Llewellyn & Co Ltd
Carlton Works
Carlton Street
Liverpool L3 7ED
Tel: 051 236 5311

Sheepskin products

Nottingham Medical Aids
17 Ludlow Hill
Melton Road
West Bridgford
Nottingham NG2 6HD
Tel: 0602 234251

Synthetic fleece (Multipad)
products – squares, heel pads and
foot comforters (slippers)

Nursey & Son Ltd   Sheepskin products
12 Upper Olland Street
Bungay
Suffolk NR35 1BQ
Tel: 0986 2821

Roussel Medical Ltd   QB2000 Heel/elbow protectors
Delves Road
Heanor Gate
Heanor
Derbyshire DE7 75J
Tel: 07737 56398

Seton Products Ltd   Tubipad, Tubifoam, fleecy boots
Tubiton House   and Parapads
Medlock Street   Synthetic sheepskin squares
Oldham OL1 3HS
Tel: 061 652 2222

Ultra Laboratories Ltd   Lyopad (egg box foam) and foam
Trinity Trading Estate   leg gutters
Tribune Drive
Sittingbourne
Kent ME1D 2PG
Tel: 0795 70953

SUPPLIERS OF COTTON AND PURE WOOL HOSE AND LARGER SIZES

Information about suppliers of 100% cotton and pure wool hose, larger sizes, heel-less sock patterns and socks without top elastic mentioned in Chapter 10 can be obtained from the Clothing Adviser at the Disabled Living Foundation (page 187). Please send SAE for information.

SUPPLIERS OF DRESSING AND WASHING AIDS

Henry Allera   'No-Stoop' lever
24 Balsdean Road
Brighton, East Sussex BN2 6PF
Tel: 0273 32640

BTL (J Moffat)   Neatfeat stocking aid
Motor Accessories
157-159 Bolton Road
Blackburn, Lancs
Tel: 0254 59202

Carters (J&A) Ltd   Long-haired shoe horn
Alfred Street
Westbury
Wilts BA13 3DZ
Tel: 0373 822203

London Showroom:
134 Brompton Road
London SW3
Tel: 01 584 6416

Homecraft Supplies Ltd   Stocking and tights gutters
27 Trinity Road   Helping Hand
London SW17 7SF   Brevetti hose helper
Tel: 01 672 7070/1789   Elastic laces
                                      'No-Bows'

Llewellyn & Co Ltd   Stocking and tights gutter
(See page 180)   Dressing stick
                                      Long handled shoe horn
                                      Elastic laces

Nottingham Medical Aids   Stocking and tights gutter
(See page 180)   Brevetti hose helper
                                      Long handled shoe horn
                                      Floor-mounted stocking aid
                                      Elastic laces

Noran Aids
89 Humber Road
Beeston
Nottingham NG9 2ET
Tel: 0602 227008

Stocking and tights gutter
Brevetti hose helper
Long-handled shoe horn

Radiol Chemicals Ltd
Stepfield
Witham
Essex CM8 3AG
Tel: 0376 512538

Elastic laces

Riker Laboratories
1 Morely Street
Loughborough
Leicestershire LE11 1EP
Tel: 0509 68181

Buff Body Scrub – long handled
back washer – can be used for feet
with Buffped foot sponge

SML Ltd
Bath Place
172 High Street
Barnet
Herts EN5 5XE
Tel: 01 440 6522

Stocking gutters

Taylor & Law
10 Yewtree Road
Acton
London W12 0TJ
Tel: 01 743 3306

Dressing stick

SUPPLIERS OF DIY TOE CAPPING KITS

Devcon ITW
Station Road
Theale
Reading
Berks RG7 4AB
Tel: 0734 302304

Devcon Flexane – 1 lb kit suitable
for several applications

Howmedica International Ltd
622 Western Avenue
London W3 0TF
Tel: 01 992 8044

AND

The Spastics Society
16 Fitzroy Square
London W1P 5HQ
Tel: 01 636 5020

Shoeguard Plastic – kit contains
mixture for 25 toecaps

INFORMATION ON ODD SIZED FOOTWEAR

Sole Mates
46 Gordon Road
Chingford
London E4 6BU
Tel: 01 524 2423

Information on obtaining odd
sized shoes and matching shoe
service. Send SAE for details.

Stockport Odd Feet
Association (SOFA)
17 Deva Close
Poynton
Cheshire SK12 1HH
Tel: 0625 87 6498

As above and can help in other
ways. Send SAE for details

Disabled Living Foundation
346 Kensington High Street
London W14 8NS
Tel: 01 602 2491 (general)
    01 602 2982 (Clothing
    Advisory Service)

List of manufacturers supplying
odd sized pairs. Send SAE for list.

SPECIALIST ORTHOPAEDIC SHOEMAKERS FOR FOAM INSERT ADAPTATION

Chiropody Laboratory
Dean Clarke House
Southernhay East
Exeter EX1 1PQ

LSB Orthopaedics Ltd
203-4 Melchett Road
Kings Norton
Birmingham B30 3HU

Oxford Orthopaedic
Engineering Centre
Nuffield Orthopaedic Centre
Headington
Oxford OX3 7LD

Royal National Orthopaedic
Hospital
Brockley Hill
Stanmore
Middlesex HA7 4LP

Appendix III

Useful Addresses

Age Concern
Bernard Sunley House
60 Pitcairn Road
Mitcham
Surrey CR4 3LL   *Tel:* 01 640 5431

Information and advice on the needs of elderly people.

Age Concern (Greater London)
54 Knatchbull Road
London SE5 9QY   *Tel:* 01 737 3456

Fact sheet on footcare and information on chiropody services in the area.

British Diabetic Association
10 Queen Anne Street
London W1M 0BD   *Tel:* 01 323 1531
Leaflets on footcare for diabetics.

British Footwear Manufacturers Federation
72 Dean Street
London W1V 5HB   *Tel:* 01 437 5573
Information on availability of footwear to meet certain foot size problems, etc.

Disabled Living Foundation
346 Kensington High Street
London W14 8NS   *Tel:* 01 602 2491 – General
                 01 602 2982 – Clothing Advisory Service

Information available from the Clothing Advisory Service on footwear and hose. Will supply the pattern for the DIY shoe (SAE).

Foot Health Council
St Leonard Hospital
Nuttall Street
Kingsland Road
London N1 5LZ   *Tel:* 01 739 8484

Health Education Council
68 New Oxford Street
London WC1A 1AH   *Tel:* 01 637 1881

Leaflets about shoes and care of young feet. Information also available for local health education officers.

Royal Society for the Prevention of Accidents
Cannon House
The Priory, Queensway
Birmingham B4 6BS   *Tel:* 021 233 2461

Advice on accident prevention.

Shoe and Allied Trades Research Association (SATRA)
SATRA House
Rockingham Road
Kettering
Northants NN16 9JH   *Tel:* 0536 516318

Specialist and technical advice on footwear; information on allergy problems.

Society of Chiropodists
8 Wimpole Street
London W1M 8BX   *Tel:* 01 580 3228

Publications on footwear and footcare.

Society of Shoe Fitters
Carlisle House
8 Southampton Row
London WC1B 4AW   *Tel:* 01 242 7017

    Advice on shoe fitting problems.

William Timpson Ltd
Timpson House
Southmoor Road
Wythenshore
Manchester M23 9NU   *Tel:* 061 998 5261

    Information on footwear and a fact sheet on difficult to find shoe sizes and fittings.

Appendix IV

Further Reading

About bedsores – what you need to know to help prevent and treat them, by Marian E. Miller and Marian L. Sachs. Philadelphia, JB Lippincott Co, 1982.

Care of the feet for diabetics, by the Society of Chiropodists, 8 Wimpole Street, London W1M 8BX (leaflet).

Foot and ankle pain, by Rene Cailliet. Philadelphia, FA Davis Co, reprinted 1970.

Footwear and footcare for disabled children, by Janet Hughes. Disabled Living Foundation, London, 1982.

Footwear for problem feet, by M. D. England. London, Disabled Living Foundation, 1973.

Geriatrics for physiotherapists and the allied professions, by Margaret Hawker. Faber & Faber, London, 1974.

How to avoid falls, Royal Society for Prevention of Accidents, Cannon House, The Priory Queensway, Birmingham B4 6BS (leaflet).

How to avoid slips, trips and falls. Scriptographic Publications Ltd, 92-104 Carnwath Road, London SW6 3HW.

Joint first aid manual, 4th ed. British Red Cross with St. John's Ambulance. Supply Department, British Red Cross, 4 Grosvenor Crescent, London SW1X 7EQ.

Provision of medical and surgical appliances handbook, 3rd ed. Blackpool, DHSS, 1983 (limited circulation).

The management and prevention of pressure sores, by Anthony Barton and Mary Barton. Faber & Faber, London, 1981.

The make-it-yourself shoe book, by Christine Lewis Clark. London, Routledge and Kegan Paul, 1979.

Appendix V

Glossary

Abduction	A movement at a joint away from the mid line of the body
Acute	A condition which has a short and relatively severe course
Adduction	A movement at a joint towards the mid line of the body
Allergy	A response which is greater than normal to the presence of a substance eaten, injected or placed on the skin
Amputation	The surgical removal of all or part of a limb
Ankylosis	The stiffening of a joint due to the surfaces being joined by fibrous tissue or bone as a result of damage, injury, or disease
Anterior	The front of a structure. (*Opposite:* posterior)
Arthrodesis	A surgical procedure in which the joint is fixed to stop movement occurring
Arthroplasty	The reconstruction of a joint by means of an operation in order to improve its function
Ball of foot	That part of the sole under the 1st and 2nd metatarsal heads
Bunion	An enlargement of the head of the 1st metatarsal bone
Bursa	A small fluid-filled sack formed to reduce friction between moveable parts of the body

190

Calcaneo-valgus	A deformity in which the foot is held in *calcaneus* and *valgus* i.e. bent up and out by a mixture of dorsiflexion and eversion
Calcaneum	The heel bone
Calcaneus	A deformity in which the foot is fixed pointing upwards and the toes cannot be put to the floor in standing
Callosity	An increase in thickness of the horny layer of the skin caused by pressure or friction, or by bearing abnormal amounts of weight
Cavus	High arched
Chilblains	Red, swollen, itchy, painful areas on fingers or toes or ears caused by extreme cold and damp
Chronic	A condition which continues over a long period or tends to reoccur
Congenital	A condition present at birth
Cramp	Painful involuntary contraction of muscle which can be due to over-use, salt loss or nerve root irritation
Cuboid	One of the bones of the *tarsus*
Cuneiform	There are 3 cuneiform bones which are part of the *tarsus*
Distal	The part at the greatest distance from a central point (*Opposite:* proximal)
Dorsiflexion	The movement of the foot and ankle upwards towards the leg (*Opposite:* plantarflexion)
Dorsum	The top surface of the foot
Equinus	A deformity in which the foot is fixed pointing downwards and the heel cannot be put to the floor when standing
Eversion	A movement in which the foot is rotated outwards until the sole is pointing away from the other foot

Evertors	The muscles which turn the foot outwards (eversion)
Exostosis	An abnormal bony outgrowth from the bone caused by pressure
Fibula	The smaller of the two bones in the lower leg
Flexion	The movement of bending or the condition of being bent
Fusion	The joining together of bone with bone
Gait	The way of walking
Hallux	The big toe
Hallux rigidus	A condition in which there is limitation of upwards movement (extension) of the big toe
Hallux valgus	A deformity in which the big toe bends sideways towards the other toes
Hammer toe	A deformity in which the toe becomes permanently bent at the joint nearest to the foot and straight at the joint at the end of the toe
Immobilise	To hold moveable parts together by means of some type of support e.g. a splint
Instep	The upper surface of the foot between the toes and the ankle
Intrinsic	A collective term given to the small muscles of the foot
Inversion	A movement in which the foot is turned inwards until the sole faces the other foot
Invertors	The muscles which turn the foot in (inversion)
Interphalangeal joints	The joints of the toes
Lateral	Situated away from the mid line of the body (*Opposite:* medial)
Ligament	A band of tough flexible fibrous tissue which attaches bones to other bones

Matrix	The nail bed – the area of the skin on which the nail rests
Medial	Situated towards the mid line of the body (*Opposite:* lateral)
Metatarsals	The 5 long bones extending from the tarsus to the toes
Motor	Concerned with movement
Muscular imbalance	The situation in which some musles are stronger than others acting on the same joint
Navicular	One of the bones of the *tarsus*
Neoplasm	New growth of abnormal cells
Neurology	The medical speciality dealing with the nervous system
Neuropathy	A term used to describe impairment of the peripheral nervous system
Oedema	Swelling
Orthosis	Device added to the body to aid function of a body part damaged, diseased or deficient
Osteotomy	An operation in which the bone is cut and re-aligned
Paralysis	The loss of the ability to move
Peripheral	Something near the surface of the body
Pes	Latin for the foot
Pes cavus	High arched foot
Pes planus	Flat foot
Phalanges	The toe bones
Plantarflexion	Movement of the foot away from the front of the leg (*Opposite:* dorsiflexion)
Plantar surface	The sole of the foot
Plantigrade	The usual position of the foot in standing with the ankle at a right-angle and the toes touching the floor
Posterior	The back or rear of a part (*Opposite:* anterior)

Pronation	A movement which combines abduction and eversion
Prosthesis	A structure added to the body to replace a deficient part such as an artificial limb
Proximal	A part situated close to the centre of the body (*Opposite:* distal)
Remissions	Periods when a disease is not active
Sensory	Relating to sensation
Sesamoid	Small bones under the big toe joint
Subluxation	A partial dislocation of a joint
Supination	A movement which combines adduction, inversion and plantarflexion
Synostosis	The joining of bones by the hardening of the connecting tissues
Systemic	A disease involving the whole body
Talipes	Description of a deformity of a child's foot
Talipes equinovarus (club foot)	A deformity in which the foot is twisted downwards and inwards
Talipes calcaneovalgus	A deformity in which the foot is twisted up and out
Talus	The highest of the tarsal bones which articulates with the leg bones (tibia and fibula) in the ankle joint
Tarsus (instep)	The region of articulation between the foot and the leg made up of 7 bones – *talus, calcaneus,* navicular, cuboid and 3 cuneiform bones
Tendon	Fibres which attach a muscle to a bone
Tibia	The shin bone
Torsion	Twisting of a bone
Traumatic	Caused by violence
Tuberosity of navicular	Part of the navicular which can be felt on the inner side of the foot
Valgus	An angulation deformity of a joint away from the mid line of the body

Varus	An angulation deformity towards the mid line of the body
Vascular	Relating to the blood supply
Vasomotor	The regulation of contraction and expansion of blood vessels

Index

Note: Entries in italics indicate illustrations where these occur on a different page from the relevant text.